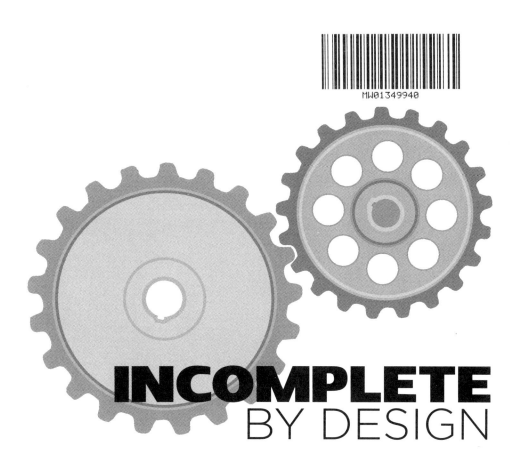

ENDORSEMENTS

Steve and Sally are proven leaders and ministers of the gospel. They write not from a theoretical point of view but as ones with authority gained through a wealth of experience in building healthy functioning teams. Not only does *Incomplete by Design* lay a biblical foundation for the necessity of team ministry, it presents practical tips on how to build a solid leadership team.

Steve and Sally highlight God's focus on relationships and bring a balanced understanding of unity. With the wise application of seasoned leaders, they explain interdependence in the body of Christ and the value of every team member's contribution. They encourage teams to operate with honor and maturity, understanding that fulfillment of each destiny lies in mutual connection. I highly recommend *Incomplete by Design* not only to new leaders building their first team but also to experienced pastors and leaders looking to strengthen their teams and organizations in preparation for revival.

DR. TOM JONES
Executive Director
Apostolic Network of Global Awakening
Overseer of ANGA
Cleveland, TN

I have walked the nations of the earth with Steve and Sally Wilson for over two decades! We have given our lives to each other just as the Bible teaches us to do. We were placed together by the Holy Spirit, knowing that He was building us into His temple. We did not join an organization to do things together, but were divinely joined, knowing that we were members together in His body and that He was shaping us into a capacity to be filled full with Himself! We knew that He wanted to mature us, and many others, into the beautiful body of our magnificent head...The Lord Jesus Christ!

I have watched and experienced the truths written in this book. Steve is not a man writing a book about some truth! He is a man who has had truth imparted into his life that has transformed him into one who has Christ living through him. He has embraced the grace given to him by Jesus. He has also embraced the grace given to others and has seen the need of that grace in his life and the life of Christ's church.

God revealed to him that we are *Incomplete by Design*. When Steve teaches these truths, I have watched The Father change lives and churches. What is the change? Christ is measuring out His fullness and His glory is seen more and more! Take the journey through this book and you will experience more fullness!

DR. SAM MATTHEWS
President of Family of Faith College
Apostolic Leader of International Connections
Author of, *Apostolic Teams: Penetrating the Nations*
Shawnee, OK

ENDORSEMENTS

Incomplete by Design is a NOW book. In this new era we will begin to experience a shift in the governmental structures of the Church from institutionalized organizations to relational organisms. The church will recover its highly relational core values. The blueprint for biblical leadership has always centered on relationship, unity, and interdependence on God and each other. From Moses, to Jesus, to the disciples; the model of effective kingdom leadership is found in team. I have met Steve and Sally's team. They are passionate, healthy, activated, and pursuing the purposes for which they were created in agreement with a bigger vision for their lives, church, city and far, far beyond. Steve and Sally write what they have lived. More than theory, they have pioneered the way and given us all a map to navigate our own leadership journey towards team in this new time.

DR. KIM MAAS
Kim Mass Ministries
Moorpark, CA

It is rare that a book will capture as many emotions in me as this one did, everything from joy to conviction, amen to oh my, and a desire to rethink our own leadership structure. If "TEAM MINISTRY" has seemed elusive or baffling to you, then this book will open your eyes to a whole new realm of understanding - a true blueprint for a functioning church leadership. *Incomplete by Design* is the product of Biblical wisdom walked out in the personal lives and experiences of Steve and Sally Wilson, whose hearts are devoted to one purpose, making Jesus King through a unified body. I cannot wait to have it in our hands. Well done!!!!

MICHAEL PEDERSEN
Pastor
Fountain of Life Church
Regina, Saskatchewan, Canada

INCOMPLETE BY DESIGN

My wife, Jean, and I treasure our relationship with Steve and Sally Wilson who we have known for more than twenty years. We truly honor their friendship and embrace the passion of their hearts — to see leadership teams in the Church work together in unity so as to reflect the harmony and beauty of the Father, Jesus and the Holy Spirit. I recommend we take time to examine the principles presented in *Incomplete by Design* and allow the Holy Spirit to show us our incompleteness. Let us ask God to connect us with people who will fill the gaps in our lives with great delight and honor. Let the passion of God in Steve and Sally's heart, as expressed in this book, be communicated to all of us.

NARASH AND JEAN SAMAROO
Apostolic Leader and Pastor
Christian Community Fellowship
Hollis, NY

When reading *Incomplete by Design*, the same phrase kept coming to my mind: "A book for days like this." Oh how the church needs to hear this prophetic voice that enables us to stand where God wants us in these very historical days in which we live as a Church. It reveals that the plan of God from the beginning is that we cannot do it alone, and for the first time allows us to enjoy ourselves being incomplete in a world that puts pressure on individuals and especially pastors and church leaders for not being able to do it all alone. Pastor Steve and Sally Wilson shared their life experience in this book saving us from spending a lifetime to learn this essential truth that we are *Incomplete By Design*. So stop trying to do it alone.

GABY EL AOUAD
Apostolic Leader and Pastor
King Jesus' Church
Beirut, Lebanon

ENDORSEMENTS

Steve and Sally's latest book *Incomplete by Design* presents a compelling and scripturally based argument for being intentionally created incomplete. This divine design reflects the plurality, unity, and perfect harmony of the Godhead. Only a culture of honor and mutual submission can sustain the now—and coming—revival. The question of women in ministry and leadership is especially addressed in a fresh and thoughtful manner. Their book corrects, encourages, and provokes us to rethink our current individualistic ministry model. I was blessed to read it and highly recommend it to all who are pursuing God's model of unity.

JOEY HAY, MA
Women's Ministries Pastor
Hope Church
Springfield, MO

Steve and Sally Wilson's book *Incomplete by Design* brilliantly reveals the biblical blueprint of team ministry. We are not created to function alone but are most effective within a family, team or group. This does not dilute our individual characteristics or gifts but instead highlights them like the colors in a rainbow. God is relational and within the Godhead exists a model of a relational community. Because we were made in His image, we were created for relationship and community. The evidence of God at work in our relationships is that He establishes family. Steve & Sally Wilson have stood the test of time in Kenya, the UK and now the US. There is a real authority about the things written in this book from their own stories, experiences and from the Word. Their deepening desire for Jesus Christ is evidence that their ministry is fruitful over a sustained period of time.

TIM ELDRIDGE
Catalyst/Connector
Senior Leader
Harrogate New Life Church
Harrogate, N. Yorkshire, UK

INCOMPLETE BY DESIGN

The Wilson's have crafted a manuscript reading more like an anthem of hope for revival than a how-to-guide for church structure. *Incomplete by Design* takes the reader on a journey through Biblical foundations and cultural ideals, establishing clear and concise concepts for today's thriving churches that are discovering their need for one another. *Incomplete by Design* combines insights to church organization, based on life-giving Biblical principles. This book gives a roadmap for those desiring an organic approach to church-life, one that is based on collaborative efforts of gifted people within the "Body of Christ." It answers many questions being asked by a generation of passionate and principled followers of Christ. The reader will find pearls of wisdom in this book, bringing expectancy and reason for being incomplete by design.

CARTER AND DIANA WOOD
Senior Leaders at Vertical Call
Santa Rosa, CA

Fascinating, revealing, revelatory and heart-searching are some of the words I think best describe *Incomplete by Design*. The heart and intent of God can be seen and experienced in reading this book. It has touched me deeply and has inspired and motivated me to rededicate my life to the building of teams and never to give up on people. Many books appeal to the soul/intellect, but this one appeals and speaks straight to the heart. It is truly an expression of the heart of Christ, soundly written with the Word as the base. Steve you are truly an Apostolic Father. I, therefore without any hesitation or reservation, recommend this book *Incomplete by Design* to every apostolic team.

P. C. WILLIAMS
Apostolic Leader
Full Gospel Fellowship
Georgetown, Guyana

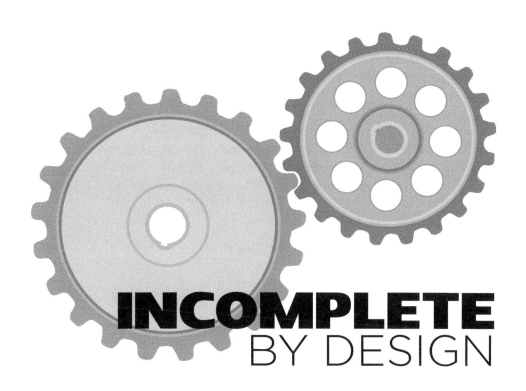

INCOMPLETE BY DESIGN

TEAM MINISTRY
A CHARACTERISTIC OF REVIVAL CULTURE

STEVE & SALLY WILSON

Incomplete by Design; Team Ministry, A Characteristic of Revival Culture by Steve and Sally Wilson © Copyright 2015 Steve and Sally Wilson. All rights reserved.

Edited by: Farley Lewis & Bob Baynard

No part of this book may be reproduced, stored or transmitted in any form or by any means, electronic or mechanical, including photocopying and recording, or by any information storage or retrieval system, except as may be expressly permitted in writing by the publisher. Requests for permission should be addressed in writing to:

Apostolic Network of Global Awakening
1451 Clark Street
Mechanicsburg, PA 17055

For more information on how to order this book or any of the other materials that Global Awakening offers, please contact the Global Awakening Bookstore.

Unless otherwise indicated, all scripture taken from the NEW AMERICAN STANDARD BIBLE®, Copyright ©1960, 1962, 1963, 1968, 1971, 1972, 1973, 1975, 1977, 1995 by The Lockman Foundation. Used by permission. (www.Lockman.org)

Scripture quotations marked (NLT) are taken from the Holy Bible, New Living Translation (NLT), copyright ©1996, 2004, 2007 by Tyndale House Foundation. Used by permission of Tyndale House Publishers, Inc., Carol Stream, Illinois 60188. All rights reserved.

THE HOLY BIBLE, NEW INTERNATIONAL VERSION®, NIV® Copyright © 1973, 1978, 1984, 2011 by Biblica, Inc.® Used by permission. All rights reserved worldwide.

Scripture quotations marked (ESV) are from the ESV® Bible (The Holy Bible, English Standard Version®), copyright © 2001 by Crossway, a publishing ministry of Good News Publishers. Used by permission. All rights reserved.

ISBN: 978-1-937467-86-9

DEDICATION

PHILIP AND MURIEL MOHABIR
Remembering the past, we honor our spiritual parents, Philip and Muriel. Together they modeled team in their marriage and taught us team in ministry. Much of the content of this book is as a result of their influence in our lives and we will be forever grateful for their friendship.

PHILIP AND HANNAH WILSON
Looking to the future, we dedicate this to our son and daughter-in-law. Hannah is the perfect helpmate for our son Philip. She completes him and compliments him as they walk into their destiny together. What a joy to watch them as a team step into their place and succeed Sally and me as lead pastors of Dayspring.

TABLE OF CONTENTS

ACKNOWLEDGEMENTS	i
FOREWORD	iii
INTRODUCTION	v

PART I - BIBLICAL FOUNDATION FOR TEAM MINISTRY

CHAPTER 1	*PLURALITY: HEAVEN'S PATTERN*	3
CHAPTER 2	*CREATION: IN HIS IMAGE*	11
CHAPTER 3	*LEADERSHIP: TEAM MODEL*	19
CHAPTER 4	*DIVERSITY: INTERDEPENDENT DESIGN*	25
CHAPTER 5	*FIVEFOLD: UNITY IN DIVERSITY*	35
CHAPTER 6	*FELLOWSHIP: OUT OF ISOLATION*	47
CHAPTER 7	*RELATIONSHIP: SUSTAINED BY THE SPIRIT*	59

PART II - PRINCIPLES FOR IMPLEMENTING TEAM MINISTRY

CHAPTER 8	*AGREEMENT: JUST ADD GRACE*	73
CHAPTER 9	*PARTNERS: FOUNDATIONS FOR TEAM*	85
CHAPTER 10	*TEAMWORK: UNITY TO UNIT*	97
CHAPTER 11	*DELEGATION: SHARED RESPONSIBILITY*	109
CHAPTER 12	*AUTHORITY: UNDER HIS RULE*	121
CHAPTER 13	*CONFLICT: OPPORTUNITY FOR GROWTH*	133
CHAPTER 14	*TOGETHER: BUILDING TEAMWORK*	145

ENDNOTES	153

ACKNOWLEDGEMENTS

We are grateful to the Dayspring leadership team who have been the workshop for much of this book. You are each a living example of the principles we have outlined; thank you!

SPECIAL THANKS TO
Farley Lewis for proof reading, editing and valuable suggestions.

SPECIAL THANKS TO
Melissa Vanderlinden for the Cover Design

A gear is perfectly designed for a specific function, but it remains incomplete until it engages with other gears to transfer motion and power. In the same way, leaders are incomplete until they engage with others, allowing each of them to fulfill their destiny.

INCOMPLETE BY DESIGN

FOREWORD

Steve and Sally Wilson's new book, *Incomplete By Design*, is not only an interesting read, it is a most practical book dealing with the subject of team building and team leadership. Steve believes that team leadership is necessary to sustain a revival, a revival culture, and a strong healthy church or business. His insights are thoroughly based upon the wisdom of the Bible. He draws from the Bible as well as the best in the field of organizational leadership. Using stories from his own life illustrates the points of the book, making them easier to comprehend. The first part of the book is more theological, revealing the intentionality of God in designing us to work in team and the importance and wisdom for working in team rather than as lone-ranger types.

The second part of the book, "Principles for Implementing Team Ministry," is the practical outworking of the theological and biblical injunction to work in team. Steve lays out a master plan for what it will take to create and sustain a great team. I found much material here that was most helpful. I believe every person whether in the church or in business could learn much wisdom from the how-to's in this section. This is the kind of book I wish someone would have given me at age 23 instead of reading it at 63. The wisdom and insights are so important to successful interpersonal relationship that are necessary for establishing a strong team.

The importance of grace, of commitment to relationship, and understanding unity and how to work as a unit were insightful. I learned much. These were then built upon in the four chapters of the book that I found so helpful. They dealt with the subjects of delegation, authority, conflict, and building teamwork. I believe the insights in these chapters are so important I hope to encourage all the pastors in our Network to read Steve's book, as well as all the students in our Global School that focuses on supernatural ministry. I believe this material could be used within teams to make them better and more productive, as well as more enjoyable and long lasting. I encourage every person who is working in relationship with others to read *Incomplete by Design*.

DR. RANDY CLARK, D. MIN., TH. D.
Founder and Overseer of the Apostolic Network of Global Awakening
Mechanicsburg, PA
Author of *There is More* and *The Essential Guide to the Power of the Holy Spirit*.

INTRODUCTION

Sally and I have been in some type of missions or pastoral ministry for over forty years. In that time we have planted and pastored churches on three continents. We have served as missionaries in Kenya, in the Comoro Islands and then in England before moving back to the US in 1991. We have planted successful churches and we have experienced dismal church failures. We have built relationships that have lasted a lifetime and had others cut short through all kinds of mischief. We have seen some of our closest friends succumb to temptation, leaving their ministry in tatters, and we have walked with others through glorious restoration.

Through all of these situations we have grown deeper in love with Jesus. We are learning to develop an unquenchable hunger for His presence. We have learned to deeply value relationships and have been forced to go to the cross and leave some there when they failed. We have also grown in our passion to see and participate in a worldwide revival. When the Lord directed us back to the US after 18 years as missionaries, it was hard to accept had it not been for the fact that He spoke of the revival that was going to sweep this nation and that He was repositioning us to be a part of it.

Over the years we had been touched by various moves of the Spirit but had not yet learned to sustain an awakening. Twenty years later we are now seeing the signs of the revival we were promised. We have had the privilege of traveling with Randy Clark in Brazil and basking in the anointing he carries for revival. We have traveled to Bethel and drunk deeply from the culture of honor that sustains the revival presence in that house. With all the glorious things we have witnessed and the changes taking place in the body of Christ, we still believe an understanding of team ministry needs to be in place for revival to sustain.

So why write this book now? Quite simply, there is a world waiting to be touched with the power of the gospel. **But on some level the message is held up or distorted by a belief structure of individualistic pursuit of ministry.**

As surely as every revival in history has been birthed in prayer, the end of each revival is marked by burnout or strained and broken relationships. For the culture of honor that sustains revival to grow unhindered, we must get a revelation of our desperate need for one another.

There are numerous examples in church history of powerful moves of God that faltered when the key leader burned out because there was no team around to help carry the weight of ministry. Evan Roberts of the 1904 Welsh revival had a physical breakdown and never regained the momentum. In Argentina in the 1950's Tommy Hicks had a remarkable crusade with thousands saved and healed, but he eventually burned out. More recently Omar Cabrera ended their meetings due to exhaustion.

The thesis of this book is that team ministry is essential to maintaining a revival culture. If this is true, then to sustain a move of God we must make a move away from traditional one man leadership models and discover the team model that has been on God's heart from creation. This model was fleshed out in the Gospels through Jesus' ministry relationships. He demonstrated this with His

INTRODUCTION

disciples by sending them out in teams. Then in the rest of the New Testament the apostles functioned in team as a continuation of Jesus' model and method.

THE MISSING LINK

Our relational mission's theology comes from Jesus' prayer: *I in them, and You in Me, that they may be perfected in unity, so that the world may know...* (John 17:23). In His request to the Father, Jesus gave us three relationships foundational to mission. To be effective we must commit to all three, keeping them present and active in our lives. The first relationship to establish is our relationship with Him; the second is our relationship with the body; and the third is our relationship to the world. These three relational spheres are dynamic tensions that we must each keep in balance.

CHRIST IN US

The first and the primary relationship is the relationship with Jesus. This relationship is the mystery of the ages - *Christ in you the hope of glory* - the King living in His subjects (Col. 1:27). How can the almighty God fit into His creation? It is a mystery! But the revelation that we're in Him and He is in us is the foundation for our passion and forms the basis for our intimacy with Him. This passion for hosting His presence becomes the controlling passion of our lives so that we no longer live for ourselves but for Him.

Paul in his letter to the Corinthians tells us that, *...the love of Christ controls us...* (2 Cor. 5:14). His motivation was to remain under the control of the King in everything. This concept does not fit neatly into our culture; we do not want anyone to control us. We like to feel we are independent and in control; but the gospel demands a surrender of our 'rights' if we are going to learn to seek first the Kingdom.

PERFECTED INTO A UNIT

Our passion for God must have an outworking in our relationship to the body. The link between our passion for God and the world being touched is the strength of our relationships within the body of Christ. Without unity in the body, the world will only see a distorted Jesus. The first and second commandments (Matt. 22:37-39) tie our relationship with God to our relationship with our brother. It is impossible to function fully in our spiritual calling without getting our relationships healed and in order.

Jesus did not speak in John 17:23 of just unity but of being perfected into a 'unit'. A unit is a group of highly trained individuals coming together to accomplish a task. The great commission calls us to go together into the nations and make disciples. To accomplish this task requires working together, learning one another's strengths and weaknesses so we can react together in any given situation. This is true team ministry - recognizing that we desperately need one another and understanding that only together are we complete. God formed us with this capacity for teamwork. We were created **incomplete by design.** To function as a unit we need the revelation that no matter how gifted we are, we need one another to complete the task we have been given.

THE WORLD WILL KNOW

The perfected unity in the body is the conduit that transmits the presence and power of God to the world. With us united, they will see a clearer image of who Jesus really is. So our purpose is not unity, but that, through the unity, the world would see Christ revealed. Our mission is to 'Make Jesus King' by becoming a true reflection of His glory and nature. Our commission is to make disciples of all nations, teaching them to relate correctly to God, to relate correctly to each other and finally to impact the world they live in with the message of Jesus. All three of these relationships are necessary if we are to fulfill Christ's commission.

When all three relationships converge, we begin to actually manifest the Kingdom. This is the "sweet spot" – the place of greatest effectiveness. I am not much of a golfer but just occasionally I will hit the ball on the sweet spot. The feel and results are amazing. With no additional effort I get distance and accu-

INTRODUCTION

racy - what a rush. The same applies to our life in mission. When we get these three relationships together, the effects are dramatic.

We see these three relationships in operation in the book of Acts. At Pentecost they were together in one place, relationships were put in order, the focus was toward heaven, and heaven responded as the Spirit fell. The result was that they went immediately out into the world, speaking the transforming power of the gospel. We have a relationship with the King and we have a commission to the ends of the earth. ***It is time to connect these with living relationships for the sake of the Kingdom.*** A desperate world is waiting!

INCOMPLETE BY DESIGN

x

PART I
BIBLICAL FOUNDATION FOR TEAM MINISTRY
WE NEED EACH OTHER

Since we are all one body in Christ,
we belong to each other
and each of us needs all the others.
ROMANS 12:5 NLT

CHAPTER 1
PLURALITY
HEAVEN'S PATTERN

The thing that you are doing is not good.
EXODUS 18:17

My first semester at Letourneau College turned into a real culture shock. I arrived on campus straight from Kenya where I had grown up and graduated from a mission school. The semester started out with an initiation week with the entire freshman class wearing cardboard cutouts of their home state; I cut out the shape of Kenya and wore it around, hoping to remain anonymous. In fact all it did was draw more attention to me, which made life even more miserable. The week of "dog days" ended with each of the freshman being unceremoniously thrown into a pond. All of us were seated on the grassy slope that surrounded the pond, waiting our turn. The dorm I was in had an unusually large group of freshman and we were almost the last in line. We watched as one at a time students from the other dorms were dragged down to the water and dunked.

At some point Dean, one of the biggest guys in our group, pointed out that we were going to get wet anyway, but we had the option of taking a whole bunch of the upperclassmen with us. Slowly the fatalism of the moment changed to anticipation as we came into agreement on a plan and waited for the perfect opportunity. The next time our tormentors were all occupied at the edge of the lake, we formed a line, locked arms and ran down the slope. The surprise attack caught them off guard and our momentum carried everyone into the water. It was totally worth it. *That one act of agreement forged us into a team* that lasted the whole four years we were together in college.

We were created to work together in this kind of radical agreement. God designed us for fellowship, with a desire for social interaction and with a need for others. We were created with the capacity and the need to form deep and lasting relationships. The unity of our fellowship and function with each other is to be a beacon of hope to a world torn apart by division. The world waits to see the church come into a perfected unity so that they can witness a fuller demonstration of the love of Jesus displayed through His body the church. We are at our best when these life-giving relationships are in place and at our most vulnerable when we are alone.

DANGER OF ISOLATION

We are familiar with the story of Elijah and the tremendous breakthrough he had on Mount Carmel. He challenged the prophets of Baal to a competition to determine who was the true God. The One who could bring down fire would be declared God. The Baal worshipers went first, and spent most of the day crying out to their god, dancing and cutting themselves. They got tired and cut up, but they never got fire. Elijah then soaked his sacrifice with water, prayed and God answered with a firestorm from heaven. Following his stunning victory, Elijah killed the prophets of Baal, but then something happened. At the moment of triumph he did something that appears uncharacteristic; he ran from Jezebel's threats. Why? Why does a man of God lose his confidence and run from the opposition?

We all have probably heard dozens of sermons taken from this passage, but we would like to suggest that the answer is found in the account of his encounter with God in the cave on Mt. Horeb. His own confession makes it clear that one of the issues that caused him to run was that he felt alone and had lost hope for real change in Israel. He made a declaration that turned on him and produced fear. He made a confession that backfired. Remember his answer to God's question, *What are you doing here?* Twice he repeated the same thing he had said in his challenge to the prophets of Baal on Mount Carmel. *I alone am left* (1 Kings 18:22, 19:10, 14). This kind of lifestyle and confession gets dangerous fast. When we feel isolated, we become vulnerable to attacks from the enemy. When it seems that no one is walking with us, we struggle alone to dispel the lies of the accuser and sometimes they overwhelm us.

In creation God established that man should not function alone in his calling. His creational intention mirrored the Godhead who demonstrates plurality between Father, Son and Holy Spirit working together in perfect harmony. Mankind, created in God's image, was to operate in the same pattern and understanding of plurality, demonstrating our need to work together in team. Elijah was the prophet of God. Although powerfully used, he still fell victim to the weakness that God has identified in all of us from the beginning - of an individual working alone.

We know that God recognized this in His servant Elijah, because He instructed him to anoint Elisha as his successor. This meant that from that time on they traveled as a team. Elijah had the companionship of Elisha and a renewed purpose as he trained and mentored his protégé. For the rest of his life he would never feel isolation again. We would like to think that part of the double portion for Elisha meant that he learned to maintain better relationships.

God's intention for each of us is that we find relationships that will stick with us as we seek to fulfill the purpose of God for our lives. David promises that, *God places the lonely in families* (Ps. 68:6 NLT). God intends that every one of us will find real relationships in the body of Christ that will walk with us and stay with us in both the good times and the bad. Ask God today to awaken your thirst for friendships and make a commitment to let the relationships you do have go deeper. Finding others to work with us in team will prove vital to our calling!

When we look at the leadership models employed in most church structures, it is utterly amazing that we take the one thing that God declared not good - **man alone** - and we make it the standard for church leadership. How can we expect the church to thrive when we take a dysfunctional model and make it our primary pattern for doing His work? We even encourage the pastors that already feel isolated as they work alone, to avoid getting too close to their people. This comes from the fear that overfamiliarity will diminish their influence, but there are many better ways to address this than further isolation. By isolating our leaders, we set them up for failure! It is our prayer that God will give each of us a revelation of His heart for a plurality in leadership so that our labor more clearly reflects the **teamwork** God desires.

PLURALITY, THE NATURE OF GOD

Team serves as more than a new or alternative leadership style. It is a corporate way of thinking, interacting and leading which comes from the heart of God. The Godhead is the original team with Father, Son and Spirit working in perfect harmony, perfect unity, and perfect order. They exist in a state of oneness and yet plurality. Then, God made man and woman in His image, so that even the process of creating male and female wove them together into a team that would more accurately reflect His nature to the world.

Now, let's go back to the days of creation to pick up a principle. One of the most striking patterns set in scripture is established in the beginning. From the first act of creation God spoke things into existence in complementary matched pairs. Each pair represents interdependent diversity so that each alone would be incomplete without the other. The first of these pairs is heaven and earth, two realms, independent in nature but interconnected in function. The next pair is light and darkness giving us morning and evening. Then sea and dry land were created followed by the sun and moon to give the appropriate light. Soon after creatures for the land and sea were created in pairs. Each duo appears as complementary pairs that work together in perfect harmony. God's final binary pair is male and female.

God's plan for this final pair clearly was more than procreation; He wanted them to serve as leadership in His creation. God commissioned the team of Adam and Eve to rule over and to subdue the earth. From the moment mankind was placed on this earth, God intended men and women to carry out His mandate to rule as a team (Gen. 1:26, 28).

We need to be careful that consequences of sin and the fall, as well as the products of cultural interpretation of scripture, do not trump God's original intention for male and female to be in leadership together. To reinforce this, in our study of revival history we have noticed that in almost every revival in history there was a significant release of women into ministry. We have also seen that the demise of revival has often been accompanied by the repression of women. We must learn to work together in team as God intended if we want to sustain revival.

Now, it would seem a straightforward matter to think of ruling in this paradise; but God also told them to subdue it as a part of their rule. Subdue has a negative connotation, implying that things would try to invade this perfect domain and must be put down. It is clearly a "not so subtle" warning that the enemy lurks in the shadows of paradise waiting to deceive. But it also serves as a warning that we must make sure of our foundation when we present truth. Much of church history has attacked the idea of women in leadership roles; as well, religious structures have rejected team as the God-given design for leadership. These preconceptions have unfortunately weakened and even disabled the body of Christ.

THE PEOPLE OF GOD

The Old Testament gives several examples of leadership teams. Even though God usually called a single individual to initiate His purpose, it seems apparent that solo leaders are not the complete working model of leadership. When Moses brought the people of God out of Egypt and into the wilderness, the initial deliverance was accomplished with a small leadership team of Moses and Aaron. However, this began to change as soon as they were free. God began to shift them from being rescued slaves, into their destiny as the people of God. As they made the transition into this new God-given identity we see a pattern change in the leadership. Joshua came on the scene and stepped up as a leader, adding breadth to the leadership structure.

Then God used Moses' father-in-law Jethro to shed more light on His divine order for leadership. Jethro watched Moses as he alone judged the affairs of the people and went to him with a question that sounds a lot like God's perspective: *Why do you sit alone?* (Exod. 18:14 ESV) A few verses later he went on to say, *the thing that you are doing is not good* (Exod. 18:17). Oh my! Jethro just repeated God's injunction over Adam. In the same way that God saw a limitation in Adam, Jethro highlights a weakness in the way Israel was being led.

Even though Moses had been obedient to God, the model of rescue would transition into the leadership model God had designed for the people who would carry the mark of belonging to Him. The solution God gave required delegating responsibility to a team who would become leaders of 10s, 50s, 100s, 1000s, (Exod. 18:21-27). Through this change God was developing a leadership team around Moses, one that protected Moses from burnout and released others into their calling as leaders. God's pattern is a plurality based on an individual's ability to care for and deal with the needs of His people. Within a short while God would give the law to Israel; so He put in place a broad plurality of leadership that would insure His standard of righteousness would be conveyed to every household and every individual.

Having established the principle of plurality, come with us back to creation to pick up another principle that further establishes the idea that we were created incomplete by design.

I remember one day as I cried out to the Lord for an answer as to why relationships felt so shallow, I heard Him say, "I wasn't going back far enough." Then He took me on a journey back to the beginning to show me something I had missed. This process revealed His intention for each of us to have lasting relationships united by a real revelation of our need for one another. So, go with us on this journey and open your heart to the Holy Spirit. Ask Him to give you a fresh revelation of what it means to walk in real relationships with your brothers and sisters in the body of Christ.

INCOMPLETE BY DESIGN

CHAPTER 2
CREATION
IN HIS IMAGE

It is not good for the man to be alone
GENESIS 2:18

After the environment of earth was set and filled with every imaginable creature, God prepared to make man and woman, the crowning glory of His creation. They would be more than just another species of animal; they would be a special work, formed by His hand and given life from His breath. They would share a unique connection to their Creator because they were made in His image. This is something special; we bare His likeness. But in what respect did God make men and women like Himself?

Theologians have long debated this issue, but we would like to suggest a few places we could look in order to catch glimpses of the image of the Creator reflected in mankind. In the Genesis account, we read that God breathed the breath of life into man and *…man became a living being* (Gen. 2:7). The word "being" can mean alive or living, but it also refers to the soul or inner being. Since our body is not the primary place that we expect to see the image of God, we should expect it to show up in our inner man. If this is the case, then we will find His image represented and manifested in and through the spiritual, intellectual, individual and relational qualities found in our inner man.

God who is Spirit created us as **spiritual** – we are distinct from the rest of creation because we were created with a spirit. As humans we are made up of body, soul, and spirit interwoven into a whole person who is uniquely aware of their Creator. We were also created as **intellectual** beings with significant mental capacities. He designed us to rationalize, to think, and reason with the capacity to make choices. God created us as **individuals** with our own personality and passions. We have been designed with expressions of individuality, which work together in such a way that we can uniquely represent Jesus and reflect His nature to the world.

Finally, as a reflection of His image, He created us as **relational** beings with ability to connect with others and with the need for real living relationships. This is consistent with the image of God, because the very essence of God is relational. Father, Son and Holy Spirit operate as three distinct persons and yet function as one in perfect relationship. So, man and woman were created for fellowship, with a capacity for relationship with God. True fulfillment only comes when we are in right relationship with others. This capacity for fellowship even extends to our emotional responses in relationship to God and with each other. This relational part of our nature is further heightened by our ability to communicate. This capacity for both written and spoken communication is one of the sharpest distinctions between man and the animal kingdom.

THE NATURE OF GOD

This relational component is further established with the name God revealed for Himself on this final day of creation. In the first five days in the narrative of creation, God revealed Himself as *Elohim* the mighty, omnipotent One - the God who spoke a word and created the vast universe and all that populated it. Elohim declared His creation good and blessed it to prosper. The name *Elohim* assumes a love and care for creation and all that was in it. But then, at the dawn of the sixth day God revealed Himself with a new name, a name that defines a much deeper and more intimate relationship with those that He created in His image.

While dealing with the creation of mankind, God revealed Himself as Jehovah, God of righteousness, holiness and love - the God of moral and spiritual attributes, while at the same time, a God who reveals Himself as a personal, living Being. Jehovah is the God of revelation who discloses Himself to man and then comes into communion with the ones He created. Jehovah is the God who makes and keeps covenants with His people. This revelation of His covenant nature means that He created us with the ability and capacity to keep covenant with Him and with each other. God designed us to work together with Him and with others in such a way that we mirror the relational fellowship of the Trinity.

This invitation to personal relationship sets a unique value for each individual. It also establishes their capacity to receive the love of the Father and then to display His love to the world around them. As a reflection of the Creator, each person is precious to God. As a bearer of God's image, each person is worth the price of redemption. We can never again see someone as valueless because of the intrinsic value God has personally assigned to each individual.

We are important to Him and have been assigned a task - dominion over His creation. God gave men and women this gift because He shaped us to be like Him. He gave us, both male and female, the authority to rule over and subdue His creation. The principles established here in God's creational order mean that both men and women were created to rule together. This is a crucial starting place for the understanding of women in ministry today.

NOT GOOD TO VERY GOOD

The story of the creation of woman began with God's declaration that *…it is not good for the man to be alone* (Gen. 2:18). Up to this point God had inspected each aspect of His work and pronounced it good. In fact on the sixth day after the creation of man and woman and giving them rule over His creation, He declared it as "very good."

The second chapter of Genesis takes a step back in the process of creation to give more insight into the sequence of this sixth day. In the time immediately after the creation of man and before woman was created there is something in this magnificent creation that is flawed, out of order, something not as it should be. Something that God said is "not good" will now become "very good."

Strong's concordance shows the wide usage of the word "good" in scripture. The many ways it is translated show a wide variety of meanings and applications, each with significance to man. In the King James Bible this word is rendered "beautiful, best, better, bountiful, cheerful, at ease, fine, glad, graciously, joyful, kindly, loving, merry, most, pleasant, pleasure, precious, prosperity, ready, sweet, wealth, and welfare." So, when God said it is not good for man to be alone, He was referring to the whole of Adam's life and purpose. Nothing he is called to do will be as it should be if he is alone. No amount of divine help will meet the need that God sees in His creation.

This was the only thing in all of His creation that was not perfect. Although man had been created in His image, something was missing. God knew that man had a need that Adam did not understand. Adam in his perfect state would have been unaware of any deficiency, but God the creator knew the capacity of His creation. He formed him to be a social being; He made man in His image with the capacity to communicate, fellowship, and enjoy creation, not just with a Superior, but also with an equal. God knew what man did not yet comprehend.

The word *alone* God uses here when He refers to Adam literally means, "only himself, by itself, or a single part." The core concept is "to be separate and isolated!" So the obvious concern was for Adam to have companionship, someone to talk with who would be an equal. He was without a companion to share fellowship and intimacy, one who could reciprocate his feelings and tap his emotions. He needed a partner who could assume an intelligent partnership with him in the task of governing creation. He also needed a mate to fulfill the mandate for procreation. Man was created with the desire to love and be loved, but there was another need that God was exposing.

Another meaning of alone carries the idea of a single part or not in parts. The word is used of a limb of the body or a branch of a vine; it is not good because a single limb cannot represent the whole body and a single branch cannot function as the whole vine. Not good because man alone cannot represent Him, the triune God, the ultimate Team. Man had been created in God's image but without the plurality of the Godhead. He was perfect, yet he was but a single unit. In order to represent the image of God he needed plurality. God is about to alter the makeup of the man He created so that Adam could represent Him more accurately.

A SUITABLE HELPER

God's answer was to make a *helpmeet* for him, a counterpart of himself. *I will make him a helper suitable for him* (Gen. 2:18). The idea of a *helper suitable*, means that she would be one like him or corresponding to him. She would be created in such a way that she would match his affections and compliment his nature and desires. This indicates that the woman would be a perfect resemblance of the man. In using the word *helpmeet* God implies neither inferiority nor superiority, but being in all things like and equal to him.

Some have understood the idea of helpmeet to mean subservice, but this is not remotely the case. The first chapter of Genesis had already stated that rule over the earth was given to both man and woman, giving no hint that she was in any way a lesser creature. God speaks of Himself being a help to Israel and Jesus presents the Holy Spirit as the Helper. Far from subservice this is an act of completion so that in man and woman combined the full image of God could be revealed. The plain truth is that Adam needed Eve and was incomplete without her. I like Matthew Henry's definition of helpmeet. "She was not made out of his head to rule over him, nor out of his feet to be trampled upon by him, but out of his side to be equal with him, under his arm to be protected, and near his heart to be loved."

INCOMPLETE BY DESIGN

Many questions come to mind at this point. Did God make a mistake? Why did He choose to make man whole then take something out of him? Why could not He just create them both at once? One thing is for certain; God knew exactly what He was doing. He knew that this process was essential to the fulfillment of His purpose for man. He wanted man to experience something that God knew but man, in his perfect state, could not yet comprehend. God wanted man to know and understand His incompleteness so that when He gave him a partner he would treat that partner as a part and completion of himself, instead of as an inferior.

What happened next can be puzzling. Instead of immediately creating woman in answer to the deficiency, God took Adam through a process of naming the animals. At first glance it looks like an exercise in dominion, acting on the mandate to rule over creation. While it may appear out of sequence, God does nothing haphazardly. In His wisdom He planned to bring Adam to revelation. He would show the perfect man He created his incompleteness by taking him through a process of self-discovery.

God was not trying to find a mate for Adam but was causing Adam to see that he needed one. God used the naming of the animals as an object lesson, a visual demonstration. The parade of animals was to show man his incompleteness, to get him in touch with an inner need of which, to this point, he had been unaware. In the act of exercising his authority in creation, he became aware of his isolation. As the animal kingdom came past him in pairs he saw that the rest of creation had a built-in plurality; there were two of each kind who worked as a team in God's mandate to fill the earth. Naming of the animals led to a result – *but for Adam there was not found a helper suitable for him* (Gen. 2:20). By the end of naming the animals, man saw what God knew all along; alone he stood incomplete.

God now had Adam ready for His master plan. He put His perfect creation to sleep and permanently disabled him. He took something out of Adam, so that never again could man alone fully represent the image of the Creator. From the part He removed, God formed an ideal partner, a flawless resemblance of man, but one who fully complemented and completed him. Eve was so splendid that when Adam saw her, he would see himself completed. Man and woman were not formed independently, because the unique nature of their inter-woven creation defined their relationship of interdependence. Without each other they were incomplete and unable to fulfill their God-given responsibility. Only together as a team could they reveal to the world the image of God. Only as a team would they act as His agent. As one of our friends once said, "Only in man and woman combined is the full image and agent of God revealed."

INCOMPLETE BY DESIGN

This principle forms an essential truth for the body of Christ today. Recognition of our incompleteness is a pre-fall principle. In other words, our need for others is not a result of the fall; it is God's original design. This principle modeled in the Godhead means that even in our best fully redeemed state, our need for others still remains as a God-ordained operating principle. We were created incomplete by design and only in team, be it husband and wife, leadership teams in the body of Christ, or as fivefold ministry teams, will we find fulfillment. This understanding of incompleteness must bring us to repentance for our independence and form in us a desperate need to find correct relationships with our brothers and sisters. In the next chapter we will see this principle fleshed out in the life and ministry of Jesus.

INCOMPLETE BY DESIGN

CHAPTER 3
LEADERSHIP
TEAM MODEL

He summoned the twelve and began to send them out in pairs
MARK 6:7

Throughout Jesus' ministry we see Him modeling team. From the first miracle in which the team member was His mother Mary, He worked with others first to demonstrate, then to equip, empower and finally to send out in teams. From early in His ministry *He appointed twelve, so that they would be with Him and that He could send them out to preach* (Mark 3:14). Notice that the call wasn't to be taught by Him (that would happen), neither was it to be an organized training program. They were being invited to be **with Him.** They shared life together; they laughed together; they ministered together; they ate together. Jesus' model for developing team had more to do with fellowship than it did with education. It has been said that education is not the filling of a pail, but the lighting of a fire. No one modeled this better than Jesus. **Being with Him lit a fire in the disciples.** Perhaps that's why we struggle to raise up leaders?

JESUS' TEAM MODEL

After His disciples had watched Him in ministry, He moved to the next step of their learning process. What He instituted with them provides a working paradigm for ministry; *He summoned the twelve and began to send them out in pairs...* (Mark 6:7). The model of God's government established in creation with Adam and Eve was now continued in Christ. As with Adam and Eve, He sent them out in pairs. The same pattern established for the first Adam was fleshed out in the last Adam. God intends us to function in leadership and ministry in His kingdom as teams. Whatever the makeup of the team, the minimum is as a pair.

Next, He sent out seventy others, *and sent them* **in pairs** *ahead of Him to every city and place where He himself was going to come* (Luke10:1). Not only were they sent out, but they also served as an advance team for His ministry. The lesson here is that a pair serves as the basic operating unit in the expansion of the Kingdom of God.

Just before the cross, while praying in the garden, He still wanted His team with Him. He chided them for being sleepy in the moment when He really needed their support. And even though they did not live up to their own expectations, He still trusted them to do the work He had trained them for. When he appeared to women after His resurrection, He told them to give a message to the disciples and Peter. He valued people even when they had let Him down. They were not disqualified! They were His team.

TEAM MODEL IN ACTS

In the book of Acts Paul and the other disciples carried on the plurality they had learned from Jesus. We see them together in teams throughout the book of Acts, whether preaching or in prison: Peter and certain brothers (Acts 10), Paul and Barnabas (Acts 13,14), Paul and Silas (Acts 15), Paul with Pricilla and Aquilla (Acts 18), Timothy and Erastus to Macedonia (Acts 19). In each of these situations we see the disciples take the lead from what they witnessed in the life of Jesus and then pass the model on to the next generation of leaders.

In chapter eight a great revival broke out while Philip was preaching in Samaria. As soon as the news reached Jerusalem the apostles were sent. Why? Did they not trust Philip? Hardly. I believe they went to fill out the message, to add their part. Do we believe that Philip had the anointing to see them come into the Holy Spirit? I think so. It was not about anointing but about team. God had established a pattern and, even if a single individual births something, His intention will always be that the other gifts are drawn in so that the full image of the Creator can be represented.

We see this design further reinforced in the fivefold ministry model. This will be covered in far more detail later, but we want to briefly touch on it here as it relates to team. We read that, *He who ascended… gave some as apostles, and some as prophets, and some as evangelists, and some as pastors and teachers* (Eph. 4:10, 11). These equipping gifts, while individually necessary to bring the body to maturity, serve interdependently in the process. When Christ ascended, we understand that He divided His fullness into five distinct ministries. Each gift is a part, and only a part of His fullness. Each of us will only ever display a part of His nature and ministry, and no single ministry has the capacity to fully express His nature. No individual gift is complete in itself. **We need one another**. In fact, each gift is incomplete by design.

For the body of Christ to come to maturity, it must be touched by all five gifts. This truth operates as the heart and soul of team. Team brings together diverse gifts based on the revelation that ***only*** when we function together are we complete. The application of this comes from the revelation of our incompleteness without one another. When we understand this, we will begin to value others in a new way. We will value one another's perspectives and seek to learn from one another's strengths. We will also be diligent to cover their weaknesses, rather than expose them. The byproduct of accepting our incompleteness will be genuine honor of one another. If we want to see Christ's fullness revealed, we must function in team.

We believe that the apostle Paul had a profound grasp of the need for team. Each time he went out someone was with him and they always ministered together. This is nowhere more evident than when he arrived in Troas. *Now when*

I came to Troas for the gospel of Christ and when a door was opened for me in the Lord, I had no rest for my spirit, not finding Titus my brother; but taking my leave of them, I went on to Macedonia (2 Cor. 2:12, 13). Read that again! Paul went to Troas with the intention of preaching the gospel. The door to preach in Troas was opened by the Lord – what a great opportunity for a whole region to hear the good news! But look what happened! Paul had unease in the spirit; for whatever reason Titus did not show up. We are not told what happened, but obviously they had planned to meet there and something delayed him. The disquiet he felt proved so profound that even with a wide open door for ministry, Paul was unwilling to "go it alone."

Think about this for a moment. What motivated this change? We know that Paul was not afraid to minister and he wasn't insecure. So what we suggest is that Paul knew that without a team, Troas would get a slightly distorted image of leadership. Paul understood that he was incomplete by himself and that the Troas church needed to be planted by a team so that they would understand the plurality of ministry necessary to bring the church to maturity.

ELDERS IN ALL THE CHURCHES

The biblical basis for plurality in local church leadership is perhaps most clearly established by the use of the word *elder*. Of the 69 times the word *elder* occurs in the New Testament, it is used twice in the singular referring to the oldest child (Luke 15:25, Rom. 9:12) and seven times it is used in the singular to describe an elder's role or position (1 Tim. 5:1, 2, 19; 1 Pet. 5:1, 5; 2 John 1; 3 John 1). The remaining 60 times it is used in the plural form to describe leadership in the local church. This is not the time or place to do an in-depth study of the concept of eldership; however, for the sake of our discussion it is crucial to recognize that the early church was governed by a plurality of elders.

Just to give a few examples, we read that the apostolic team ordained elders in every church (Acts 14:23). We are told that the elders were to rule well (1 Tim. 5:1). The sick were to call the elders of the church to come and pray for them and to anoint them with oil (James 5:14). The elders of the church were to oversee the flock of God (1 Pet. 5:1-5). Relief money was sent to the elders in the church (Acts 11:30). Clearly, the local church in the New Testament was governed by a plurality of elders.

Even when an apostle, a prophet or other fivefold gift was present in the leadership team, it is clear that they still considered themselves part of the local leadership plurality. Peter, who had just introduced himself as an apostle, went on a few verses later to call himself a fellow elder (1 Pet. 5:1). So even though one of the fivefold ministry gifts present in the church may well have been the team leader, it appears that they operated as fellow elders with co-equality in terms of responsibility. Yet they recognized that God had set within the team, a leader who some have referred to as the "first among equals."[1]

HEADSHIP AND TEAM

This "first among equals" leadership model within the eldership team was set in creation. We were made in the image of God and we have seen already that the Godhead provides the model for team. It also provides the baseline for headship. Scripture leaves little doubt that the Father serves as the leader in the Godhead. Jesus acknowledged the Father's headship repeatedly and the Holy Spirit submits both to the Father and the Son. In fact, every other team we have looked at so far in this chapter has a clear leader. We do not question the need for a head in the team; we question the wisdom of a head without a team.

Those who teach a pure plurality with no headship use as their model the church in Jerusalem. They propose that the apostles functioned as a plurality with no clear indication that there was a designated leader in the team. However, we believe that we get more than a hint that there was a leader in the team when we study Acts chapter fifteen. In what we have come to know as the "council in Jerusalem" there was a great debate as to whether the customs of the law should be imposed on Gentile believers. It appears that everyone had his say and finally, James summed it all up and issued the ruling.

This process is consistent with Semitic cultures that are elder-led. In these environments the elders all have their say and when they have finished, the most senior or the appointed leader sums up all that has been said. I remember well going to resolve a conflict in Kenya over some equipment that had been donated. Someone from outside had stepped in and legislated what should happen. Even though it was not necessarily a bad decision, it so violated the culture that it was not accepted and the whole situation threatened to blow up.

When I arrived, tempers were on edge and after a good night's sleep, we sat down with all the parties involved. For two days they all shared their thoughts, feelings and frustrations. At the end when they had all shared, the most senior pastor gave his opinion. His ruling ended up being exactly what the previous leader had tried to impose; but this time, when their leader shared it, everyone present accepted it as the way forward. The problem stemmed not from the truth of the situation but from the need to follow the correct cultural process for making decisions.

This appears to be exactly what happened at the council of Jerusalem. Each one spoke their mind and then James summed it up. Once the decision came, they all bought into the corporate decision. Even Peter who had acted as the spokesperson after Pentecost and certainly had some measure of senior leadership within the apostolic team readily submitted to the ruling that James brought. In our understanding, this makes James the recognized leader in the local church in Jerusalem. Other apostles had other areas of leadership responsibility but James served in some capacity as team leader at the home base. So where did this all change?

CHAPTER 4
DIVERSITY
INTERDEPENDENT DESIGN

So we, who are many, are one body in Christ
ROMANS 12:5

Early in the fourth century, after the somewhat dubious conversion of the Emperor Constantine, the nature of Christianity went through a dramatic alteration. For almost 250 years followers of Jesus within the Roman Empire had experienced multiple waves of intense persecution. Living under this tyranny, believers were deeply committed to their faith and no one dared visit a Christian gathering unless they were genuinely interested in following Jesus. To be a believer in Rome meant being willing to die rather than renounce their faith.

The life of a Christian centered in the home with fathers taking responsibility for training their children in the faith. The church was not built around meetings but around the family units, which made Christian *life* the focus. This model of church depended on paternity as a means of communicating the message of the gospel. Families would rehearse together the history, the values, and the culture of life in Jesus. Fathers and mothers modeled the Christian life, making it relevant to the lives of their children and extended family.

INCOMPLETE BY DESIGN

When Constantine became a patron of Christianity, the church found a new acceptance in Roman society. He first legalized the church, which meant that over the next half-century believers became integrated into Roman society. Eventually, the church became so influential that in 380 AD Christianity became the official religion of Rome under the emperor Theodosius. Throughout this period thousands joined the church, because it was now the expedient thing to do. No longer were the Christians hated and feared; in fact, if you wanted to get ahead in business or in society, you needed to join the church. It provided the context where you could network and make all the contacts necessary to do business.

This institutionalization of the church lowered the bar of radical commitment as it morphed into a more socially accepted status. This newfound favor moved the church away from its relational roots; to the point that it became more of an organization than a living organism. Spontaneous committed relationships vanished and meetings took their place. Because many of those who joined the church were at best nominal in their faith, they had little knowledge of the Scriptures and could not train their families in the Word of God. So they turned to the church to fill the void. Consequently, the model of fathers training their children was replaced with professional clergy who would do the job for them.

This profound shift in the function of leadership in the local church instituted a clergy/laity divide that still exists to this day. It also marked the move away from plurality of eldership as the form of church government. In its place a one-man leadership format began to emerge and any understanding of team ministry was lost or abandoned. After this point in history, as the church was further institutionalized, even the idea of the need for diverse ministry gifts working together to bring the church to maturity seems to have vanished.

The very nature of the church also shifted as more of church life took place in buildings than in homes. This moved the church out of the community and into special buildings that then became identified as "the church." We still struggle with this differentiation today. In the early church it was the people in a locality who made up the church; we must recapture this! Building the church has never been about filling buildings; it is about building people into fellowship with God and with each other. The church is the body of Christ, a living organism made up of people; it is not a building.

ORGANIZATION OR A LIVING ORGANISM

Paul uses the metaphor of the body to describe the church as a complex combination of thousands of parts working together to fulfill a common purpose. To the Corinthians he writes, *now all of you together are Christ's body, and each one of you is a separate and necessary part of it* (1 Cor. 12:27 NLT). Think about the incredible diversity and inter-relationship of each part. Paul affirms the value and necessity of each individual member, and then points out the need for correct alignment to the other parts, which enables the proper function of the whole body. The context of this discussion on the body is a correction of the Corinthians' focus on individual giftedness. He is calling the church back to a corporate, collective understanding. Paul's emphasis is that if we focus on individual giftedness, we will miss our purpose, but if we can come to see our gift and calling in the light of others, we will grow to maturity.

The human body provides an illustration of the incredible uniqueness of each individual part. At the same time it clearly demonstrates the inherent incompleteness of any part in isolation from the rest of the body. If we were to see a hand lying on the sidewalk, our first response wouldn't be, what a good-looking hand. No, we would immediately think that someone had lost a hand. The hand in the context of the body looks good, but separated from the arm it is grotesque. The hand is materially and functionally incomplete and useless without its connection to the rest of the body. It has no life and no purpose unless it is attached to a body. Additionally, the body it once belonged to is now disabled, because it lost a hand. This truth as it applies to the body of Christ is the theme for this book; we are designed incomplete, because we were created to need one another.

ONE BODY, MANY MEMBERS

In his letter to the Corinthians Paul had a lot to say about the makeup of Jesus' glorious body, the church. He wrote, *For even as the body is one and yet has many members, and all the members of the body, though they are many, are one body, so also is Christ* (1 Cor. 12:12). The first thing we see here is the tension between the individual and the corporate. There is a clear unity of the body and yet there is a distinct individuality of each part. The body imagery in no way calls for conformity to each other but rather a call that each be conformed to Christ the Head. Individuality, and not conformity, is fundamental to the body, because it expresses the plurality of the ministry and the multifaceted nature of Christ's character.

INDIVIDUAL UNIQUENESS

When we begin to grasp the diversity of the parts represented in the body, we get a glimpse into the unlimited creativity of our God. The more we look at and value the body, the more we recognize that uniqueness is an essential ingredient for the body to function. Continuing his treatise on the body, Paul again wrote,

> *For the body is not one member, but many. If the foot says, "Because I am not a hand, I am not a part of the body," it is not for this reason any the less a part of the body. And if the ear says, "Because I am not an eye, I am not a part of the body," it is not for this reason any the less a part of the body. If the whole body were an eye, where would the hearing be? If the whole were hearing, where would the sense of smell be?* (1 Cor. 12:14-17)

If all parts were the same, what kind of body would we have? Each part is necessary. Each member has a function. God has uniquely created every component so that they can come together as one and yet have the individuality of

DIVERSITY INTERDEPENDENT DESIGN

many members. No part is redundant; each has its role and purpose. No part can say it does not need the others. We come together as one in the body in such a way that there are no barriers. There is no room for division; there is no room for jealousy. *For just as we have many members in one body and all the members do not have the same function, so we, who are many, are one body in Christ, and individually members one of another* (Rom. 12:4, 5). This means that we belong to one another, even though our functions are all unique. In fact it is Biblically impossible to fulfill our function and calling in God without connection to the body. Interconnection is God's design for us. Catch the significance here; we cannot fulfill our destiny without connection to the other parts of the body. **They are necessary parts of our individual development!**

Perhaps more startling, particularly for us in today's consumer culture, is that God places us as He desires. We do not choose where we go or where we fit. *God has placed the members, each one of them, in the body, just as He desired* (1 Cor. 12:18). He places us! Wrap our mind around this. We do not get to choose where we go, where we live, or even where we worship. God chooses for us based on His infinite knowledge of the environment that will cause us to thrive. We remember well when God called us to Springfield, MO. We knew we had heard His voice, but the circumstances of the first couple of years had us asking…why? Today, we can look back and see His hand, but it took several years for His plan to unfold.

INTERDEPENDENT DESIGN

God places us together so that we are neither independent nor dependent. God's design calls us is into interdependence. When we are interdependent we can function freely in our individual roles, while at the same time, recognizing our desperate need for one another. We come to understand that we are incomplete without others. God designed this interdependency to flow from an ability to honor the diversity in each part. *It is much truer that the members of the body which seem to be weaker are necessary; and those members of the body which we deem less honorable, on these we bestow more abundant honor…God has so composed the body, giving more abundant honor to that member which lacked* (1 Cor. 12:22-24).

By design, each part receives honor and in fact the more insignificant the part the more honor it is to receive. Many church cultures have this backwards. While there is an honor for leaders, God's design is that leaders take the lead in showing honor to the whole body (Rom 12:10). This enables us to bridge the cultural, racial, generational and socioeconomic gaps in our society. *So that there may be no division in the body, but that the members may have the same care for one another. And if one member suffers, all the members suffer with it; if one member is honored, all the members rejoice with it* (1 Cor. 12:25, 26). Read that again, there should be no division in the body.

The next verse explains why this is so important! *You are Christ's body…* (1 Cor. 12:27). **We are the body of Christ and His body is not divided**. This principle of the value of the individual is what makes a team function. The more we understand the power of releasing each individual to function at his or her full potential the more effective the team. Because this is by God's design, it works both in the natural and in the spiritual realm.

Henry Ford moved the car industry from individually built to mass produced. The power of this system capitalized on the strengths of his employees and covered their weaknesses. Each individual did one job well so they could work in an area where they were gifted. They learned to do their work and to trust others to do the next job. As a result they all became faster and more efficient with fewer mistakes. The effectiveness of team solved many of the problems facing the automotive industry. The consistency Ford achieved in the product caused an explosion in vehicle ownership, usage and reliability. The consistency also allowed the car parts industry to flourish, which lowered the cost of making the whole product more accessible

DIVERSITY INTERDEPENDENT DESIGN

FITTED AND HELD TOGETHER

Honor works by focusing on the value of the individual parts of the body that God has placed around us. Each part not only has a function, it has a supply that we need in order to fulfill our purpose. *From whom the whole body, being fitted and held together by what every joint supplies, according to the proper working of each individual part, causes the growth of the body for the building up of itself in love* (Eph. 4:16). As we receive and interact with the parts of the body around us, we are fitted together; rough edges in our character get shaved off. We are literally held together by our need for one another. We recognize that the supply for the entire body comes through the joints - the connection between believers. But the strength of these connections must go beyond our need for one another.

To the Colossians Paul wrote, *and not holding fast to the head, from whom the entire body, being supplied and held together by the joints and ligaments, grows with a growth which is from God* (Col. 2:19). Not only are we held together by the supply that flows through the joints, the joints are actually bound together by ligaments. In the natural, ligaments are what hold the joint together so the hand does not fall off. Remember, God is a covenant-keeping God and He has created us in His image with the capacity to make and keep covenants. It is His intention that we first and foremost hold fast to the Head – our source of life and direction. When Christ's headship is established, the church will grow with a growth that is from God. But for the growth of the body to sustain, we must also walk with our brothers and sisters in committed relationships. We are quite literally built together.

THE BUILDING METAPHOR

Paul used the metaphor of the physical body to correct the apparent over emphasis on individual giftedness. But he hasn't run out of metaphors. He also uses a building as a metaphor to describe the process of being fitted together with the goal of becoming a dwelling place for the Holy Spirit.

Again to the Corinthians he writes, *For we are God's fellow workers; you are God's field, God's building* (1 Cor. 3:9). The building speaks of God's structure or pattern. Christ is the foundation and individual members of the body are built together to form the structure. This does not refer to a physical building but to that living, dynamic community that exists when the people of God are correctly built together, creating a dwelling place for the Holy Spirit.

In the same way that Christ is the head of the body, He is also the foundation of the building. In construction the foundation determines the extent of the structure, the taller the building the deeper the foundation. Stability, strength and durability all depend on the unseen but indispensable foundation. In the church that foundation is Christ. It is not built on a doctrine or a philosophy but on the Person, Jesus Christ Himself. *For no man can lay a foundation other than the one which is laid, which is Jesus Christ* (1 Cor. 3:11).

To the Ephesians Paul changed the metaphor slightly and shows Christ as the corner stone. *Having been built on the foundation of the apostles and prophets, Christ Jesus **Himself** being the corner stone* (Eph. 2:20). Everything starts from that point. Jesus initiates the building; He establishes the foundation and serves as the cornerstone. Paul tells us that *according to the grace of God which was given to me, like a wise master builder I laid a foundation, and another is building on it. But each man must be careful how he builds on it* (1 Cor. 3:10). We are not building based on a denominational structure but on the foundation of Jesus; He provides the pattern, so everything that we say or do as we build is to reflect His nature and show His Glory. In fact the Church is not our church; it belongs to Him. When we begin to believe it is ours, we take it out of His hands and it all becomes hard work. He says that He will build it; so we must let Him. He promises, *I will build My church; and the gates of Hades will not overpower it* (Matt. 16:18).

In the same way that the parts of the body were fitted and held together, now in this new metaphor we get a glimpse into the process it takes to build the building. Peter calls us living stones; *you also, as living stones, are being built up as a spiritual house for a holy priesthood...* (I Pet. 2:5). Most of the buildings on the mission station in Africa where I grew up were built with quarried stone. The first thing the stonemason did before he began to shape the stone was to tap it with his hammer to check the sound. If the stone had a dull sound, it got rejected; but if it rang or sang, it was selected as a living stone and entered the shaping process.

Individual stones were first shaped in a quarry where unwanted chunks and rough edges were chiseled off to get a rough shape. Then a craftsman cut, shaped and prepared the surface of the stone to get it ready for the building. This process required precision, because many structures, including Solomon's temple, were built with dry joint masonry - sometimes called friction joints. These amazing joints tend to last longer than mortar joints, because they are less susceptible to erosion. The friction created from the contact a stone makes with the adjacent stones holds dry joints together. So, if a connection was going to hold, it needed to have a maximum surface area touching the next stone. This is achieved by making the surface of the stones perfectly smooth. Every lump, bump and imperfection is chiseled away so that the stones literally adhere to each other when they are brought into contact.

The church as a building is constructed with friction joints. Paul's description of the building process bears that out. *In whom the whole building, being fitted together, is growing into a holy temple in the Lord* (Eph. 2:21). God is building something spectacular and He is shaping us to be ready for it. Do you feel the lumps and imperfections being chiseled off? Is there friction when you rub up against your brother or sister in Christ? Take heart! You are being prepared to fit correctly in the house of God. You are being shaped so that the building under construction can house a move of the Holy Spirit. In this context growth comes as the believer interacts with others who look, think, and act differently. We can only learn to love as Jesus loves when we are put to the test through interactions with others and choose to respond correctly. This interdependent function produces unity, both real and sustainable.

This temple then becomes the dwelling place of the Holy Spirit. In the Old Testament the Holy Spirit was transitory, but in Jesus He came and remained. Now since Pentecost the Spirit has a permanent dwelling place not only in the individual but also in the corporate body. *In whom you also are being built together into a dwelling of God in the Spirit* (Eph. 2:22). The Holy Spirit has the responsibility of dispensing the love of God. So, the more correctly we are built together the more fully the love of God will be at work in and though our lives.

God established the leadership model necessary to bring the various parts of the building together. Christ instituted this pattern in His ministry and then released His ministry gifts into the church. The church is designed to be a living organism maintained by the life of the Spirit and brought to maturity by these ministry gifts Christ instituted. Their function is to equip and release each individual to do the works of Jesus and carry His message to the world.

As leaders, we have seen the need for other leadership gifts to be around us to more fully represent Jesus to the church and the world. Now we will see that the apostle, prophet, evangelist, pastor and teacher are all essential to see the church develop to maturity. Each of these offices is unique, with different strengths and weaknesses, and this is precisely what makes team ministry effective (and difficult!). This is the focus of the next chapter.

CHAPTER 5
FIVE-FOLD
UNITY IN DIVERSITY

Built upon the foundation of the apostles and prophets
EPHESIANS 2:20

The thesis of this book is that we are created "incomplete by design." This means that to fulfill our purpose we must find one another and learn to work together. Nowhere is this diversity of design more evident than in the ministry gifts Christ released to the church after His ascension. The biblical concept of fivefold ministry gives a powerful model of the diversity necessary to accomplish the task of bringing the church to maturity in order that the nations can be reached with the message of the gospel. If any part of this model is ignored or rejected, the church is at least partially disabled and unable to fulfill her mission.

All seem to agree with three of the five ministry gifts: pastors, teachers and evangelists. But when it comes to the apostles and prophets some have a problem accepting that they still exist. Whether this rejection comes from a theological position, religious tradition or just plain fear, the results are the same. The church has suffered because some of the ministry gifts designed by God Himself have been held back, and this deficit has left the church weakened. When we reject Christ's ministry gifts, we lose.

First, let me tell you my story. I first heard the term apostle used for someone other than the 12 and Paul when we served in Kenya as missionaries. It came as such a shock to my theology that I can tell you exactly where I was when it happened. I had agreed to drive Bryn, a guest speaker from England, to a meeting in Nairobi. We had been in the car only a few minutes, when I asked him a question about his ministry gift. I cannot remember why I asked, but I will always remember his answer.

"I am an apostle."

My response was anger! I remember wanting to stop the car and let him out, but I could not because we were crossing a dam and there was nowhere to pull over. I grew up with a love for the Word of God and was taught that there was no such gift today. The arrogance of his declaration offended me and I told him in no uncertain terms that I could not agree with him. He did not try to defend himself; he only asked that I go home and read through the New Testament and count how many times the word apostle is used in connection with people other than the 12. I took the challenge, not realizing that what I would discover had the potential to alter the course of our lives and ministry.

That night I pulled out the concordance and set out to prove him wrong. To my alarm the further I dug, the more distraught I became. I realized that much of what I had believed had no basis in Scripture. I think I found about 15 references the first time through and have since realized that the number is over 30. But it was not the number that scandalized me; it was the word "until" that leapt out at me as I read Ephesians. Paul answered a question I had never asked about the continuation of all the ministry gifts.

> *And He gave some as apostles, and some as prophets, and some as evangelists, and some as pastors and teachers, for the equipping of the saints for the work of service, to the building up of the body of Christ;* **until** *we all attain to the unity of the faith, and of the knowledge of the Son of God, to a mature man, to the measure of the stature which belongs to the fullness of Christ* (Eph. 4:11-13).

Christ gave the gifts, plural, **until** we attain to the unity of the faith, **until** we reach the knowledge of the Son of God, **until** we mature, **until** we reach the measure of the fullness of Christ. All of this is still in process no matter our eschatology. It is clear that we have not attained to the unity of the faith; we have not reached the full knowledge of the Son of God; we are not yet matured, and we have not reached the measure of the fullness of Christ. How could I have missed this? I remember a few days later asking for Bryn's help, because the Word of God had shattered my paradigm of a pastor-led church.

It is amazing how we can read a scripture over and over and not see something. Then in a moment the Spirit will show us what we had not seen before. Since that season I have met many who have called themselves apostles. Some liked the title but had little to show for it. Others liked the position and exercised an authority that smelled of control. Others have sought to live in such a way that the full image of Christ would be seen through them. For all those pioneers who broke the ground for us, I am truly grateful.

APOSTLES AND PROPHETS

In his letter to the Ephesians, Paul spells out the vital role of apostles and prophets. He writes, *having been built upon the foundation of the apostles and prophets, Christ Jesus Himself being the corner stone* (Eph. 2:20). He emphatically states that the church was to be built with Christ as the cornerstone and with apostles and prophets as part of the foundation-laying process. I could not escape it; my limited understanding and the religious baggage of my cessationist upbringing had duped me. Now before you stone me, I love my roots. They gave me a love for and dependence on the Word of God for which I will always be thankful. But the models for leadership I witnessed emerged from tradition and not good biblical exegesis. As I studied, I realized that God had a design for leadership much broader than I had imagined.

When the apostles and prophets are removed from the leadership equation, the church automatically turns inward. The pastor focuses on the people, the teacher focuses on the Word and the evangelist tries to keep the church turned to outreach. In practice this means that the evangelists find themselves relegated to a traveling role because they do not fit comfortably into a model that is primarily inward looking. The church led by a strong pastor/teacher will tend to drift into a fortress mentality, focusing primarily on caring for the people and results in little impact on society.

One day in reading the church fathers I ran across a quote from Novatian written somewhere around 270 AD. He was writing on the Trinity and the key role of the Holy Spirit in empowering the Church. But in the context, he also listed several of the fivefold ministry gifts including the prophet.

> *They were henceforth armed and strengthened by the same Spirit, having in themselves the gifts which this same Spirit distributes, and appropriates to the Church, the spouse of Christ, as her ornaments. This is He who places prophets in the Church, instructs teachers, directs tongues, gives powers and healings, does wonderful works, often discrimination of spirits, affords powers of government, suggests counsels, and orders and arranges whatever other gifts there are of charismata; and thus make the Lord's Church everywhere, and in all, perfected and completed.*[2]

The effects of removing the apostolic and prophetic voice from the process of building the church produce a powerless body with limited hearing. It needs the apostolic to know how to build and the prophetic to point the way. The church needs apostolic government and order, and it needs the prophetic to hear from heaven with clarity so that heaven's will is done here on earth. The church needs apostolic to release signs and wonders so that the power of the kingdom is demonstrated. Clearly there have been ministry gifts that have operated in these anointings; we simply have not called them by their true identity. But when we remove the name we remove the expectation of transformation that comes with them. When we restore these gifts to their rightful place, the foundation is strengthened and the body begins to mature.

With this new understanding it was impossible for me to go back to traditional missionary work as we had known it, and we began to ask God for clear direction. We wanted to see God do all that we saw Him do in scripture; we wanted to live in the fullness of the Spirit; we wanted to learn to use the gifts of the Spirit, and we wanted to understand how the concept of team ministry worked in practice.

In His wisdom God had a plan. A friend of ours, Mike, needed an engineer to help him develop a new design for a windmill. Most water available in our part of Kenya required a diesel engine to power the pump and Mike wanted to replace these with wind power. Through a sovereign act of God our mission seconded us to the project and we moved from the desert to Thika, a small town near Nairobi.

With this secondment came the opportunity to work under apostolic authority. We were asked to pastor the church on the farm where we lived and for the first time found ourselves free to operate in the gifts of the Spirit. We stepped almost immediately into a season of great growth. With the presence of the Holy Spirit, the anointing increased, releasing the miracles, followed by salvations. We soon moved into revival with prayer meetings going long into the night and baptisms at midnight, because there wasn't enough time in the day to get it all done. This season ended when we were called before the mission board and asked to sign a statement that we would never again speak in tongues in public. Because we couldn't sign the paper, our work permit was revoked and we were forced to leave Kenya.

GOD'S WAY OF LEADING

Paul gives definition to God's design for leadership in his letter to the Ephesians. He explains that after Christ's ascension, *He who ascended...gave some as apostles, and some as prophets, and some as evangelists, and some as pastors and teachers* (Eph. 4:10, 11). These equipping ministry gifts are not about what we are doing for God, but what He is doing through us. Each one represents an aspect of His ministry lived out through us; so no matter how magnificent the individual ministry, it is still only a part. In fact each of the five gifts is incomplete by design. Only when they work together will the body grow and develop to maturity. Too often these ministries have been taken as titles or viewed as positional. While there is positional authority within the ministries, this misses a main point in Paul's passage.

Christ who lived as the perfect apostle, prophet, pastor, evangelist, and teacher divided His ministry so that no individual gift or ministry could ever fully represent Him (Eph. 4:7). He designed leadership in such a way that each gift desperately needs the others in order to accomplish its purpose. Rather than reacting against the diversity inherent in this design, each gift should rejoice in looking to the others, recognizing the limitation of their incompleteness. Dr. Sam Matthews states that, "there is a wholeness or completeness that is achieved when they are working together. Each ministry gift is distinctive, yet while functioning together, they express more than just the sum total of the parts."[3]

Christ, the complete leader, divided Himself and trusted His ministry as a leader to human beings. The glory of this is that we have the privilege of representing a facet of His life and ministry. The caution at the same time is that no individual gift or ministry can ever fully represent Him (Eph. 4:7). Just as the bride for the first Adam was formed by taking something out of Adam, the bride for the Last Adam, Christ, is to be formed by the ministries He took out of Himself. They then work together in harmony to perfect the bride and make her ready for the bridegroom. Only when they work together will the body grow to maturity.

Some point to the apostle Paul as an example of one who had the ability to go it alone and certainly he had tremendous gift and revelation. God entrusted him with the responsibility for much of the New Testament. If anyone could have done it, it would have been him. The apostolic gifting can and does carry a breakthrough anointing and can stand alone if necessary; however, its great strengths produce corresponding weaknesses.

One of the only times that Paul ended up ministering alone was in Athens. He left Berea in a hurry, leaving Silas and Timothy behind. Those helping him get away took a message back to his team asking them to make their way to Athens to join him. However, while Paul was waiting for the team to arrive, he began to get provoked by all the idolatry he encountered in the city (Acts 17:16).

Stepping out on his own, he taught in the synagogue and debated in the public square. He eventually ended up in front of the city council defending his message about the "Unknown God." Although there were some who responded to the message, many mocked and it is the only time where it is recorded that people laughed at him (Acts 17:32).

Everywhere else he went, he traveled with a team. We find him partnering with Barnabas and then Silas. He seemed to understand that a gospel presented by only one gift, no matter how significant, would present a distorted or one-sided gospel. It would lay into the foundation of the church an individualism that would weaken the structure. The foundation by God's design comes from both the apostolic and prophetic gifting. Even though it has historically proved possible for the apostolic gifting to represent the other gifts, it gives an incomplete picture. Gifts in isolation fall short of God's intention for working in team.

This God-designed interaction allows each ministry to see the mission through the eyes of diverse gifts. Its breadth breathes new life into the body of Christ, because in valuing diversity, the relationships become strong enough to bridge cultural differences. The gifts of Christ are given to the Church as an extension of God's grace. The ministries can only function in that grace by extending grace to others through honoring those with different gifts. Philip Mohabir, who we had the privilege of knowing as a spiritual father, described the interaction of these diverse gifts.

INCOMPLETE BY DESIGN

> *The Lord knows we cannot be left to our own devices to get the job done. Therefore, He gives teams of gifted ministries composed of different people, different personalities, different experiences and different gifts. Our unity is expressed in diversity. In His infinite wisdom He gives five different ministries to be united as one and demonstrate the same quality of unity that is between the Father and the Son.[4]*

While a single individual may well operate comfortably in two or even three of the gifts, it is inconceivable that any individual would fulfill all five. This would be a complete violation of the principle. Personally, I am called as an apostle, but my internal motivation is as a pastor. I can teach, and though I enjoy teaching on occasion, I would not call myself a teacher. I am not a prophet, though I can and do prophesy when in a situation in which it is needed. I am not an evangelist, though some occasionally get saved when I minister. However, the ability to represent a ministry gift is in no way a substitute for the real thing.

We have met few people who operate strictly as one gift. Most people we have spoken with seem to manifest two of the ministries, one as a calling and another as the internal motivation or default setting. The others are simply missing. God has designed leadership in such a way that each gift desperately needs the others in order to accomplish its purpose. Rather than reacting against the diversity inherent in this design, each gift should rejoice in looking to the others, recognizing the limitation of our own incompleteness and celebrating the completeness found in diversity.

Like a great jigsaw puzzle the picture only becomes clear as the pieces come together. It is hard to see much of the image of Christ or the glory of His kingdom when our only perspective is what we see, know and have experienced. When we find connection to others, the image begins to fill out. We recognize new facets of Christ's nature fleshed out in people with different graces and expressions. As we embrace and honor this great diversity, we see the image of

Christ fleshed out through our relationships. How arrogant we were to believe that alone we could represent One so magnificent.

As the great variety of gifts and ministries begins to function together, the world around us sees a clearer picture of Jesus. Rather than the myopic image presented by any individual gift, God's designed interaction of various gifts and ministries presents a fuller picture of His nature and purpose. This magnificent design breathes new life into the body of Christ as each gift does its part. As teams of ministries learn to flow together, connections are made across every ethnic and linguistic barrier and the Church of Jesus spans the globe with a network of relationships, which reflect the glory of God.

UNITY IN DIVERSITY

A persistent confusion that has discredited the idea of fivefold ministry is that the gifts are seen as positional titles. Never in scripture does the word apostle precede the name of the individual. Rather, it always follows, because it describes the job they do, instead of a title they hold. This is true of all five of the ministry gifts. Pastor is not a title; it is a job description. It describes the gift that focuses on caring for the sheep, feeding them, tending them, and dealing with threats that seek to destroy. Evangelist is not a title; it is a job description of one who not only evangelizes, but also has the anointing to equip others to share the good news. The same with the teacher, though it is intriguing that you almost never see a business card with teacher as the title for the ministry.

These job descriptions of Christ are given to the Church as an extension of God's grace, and they can only function fully in that grace by extending grace to others. If it is true that when Christ ascended He divided His fullness into five distinct ministries, then each gift is a part, and only a part, of who He is. No individual gift is complete in itself; **we need one another**. The goal of unity can only be achieved through the correct application and understanding of this diversity. The body of Christ needs the revelation that **only** when we function together are we complete. The application of this will bring us to a unity that is real and not contrived.

We like to use the five senses as an illustration when teaching the fivefold, because they demonstrate the profound diversity of the function and operation of each ministry gift. We relate the apostle to sight because they see the big picture and have an understanding of the master plan. Hearing represents the prophet; they hear the direction well and communicate it to the body. The sense of touch could be likened to the evangelist, who touches individuals with the message of the gospel. The pastor smells the messes and knows how to clean them up. And finally, the teacher knows the sweet taste of the Word and feeds it to the body. If these ministry gifts really are this diverse, can we see how desperately we need to work in team with one another?

STRENGTHS AND WEAKNESSES

The ministry gifts share many things in common but each uniquely expresses a facet of the nature of Christ. To help us grasp the differences and the interaction between the ministries let's look at a short description of each. For each we have sought to give a brief definition, the motivation behind the gift, the viewpoint or perspective, the desire and finally the danger of isolation. We have deliberately set each in contrast to the others and do recognize that the distinctions are never this stark, but we do it this way for the sake of understanding and recognizing the amazing diversity of God's design. We also want to emphasize the truth that these ministries were never meant to operate in isolation.

An **apostle** thinks expansion of the Kingdom of God. They look at the church as a whole and are motivated to develop all the ministries in order to extend the impact of the body of Christ. Apostolic perspective can be characterized by overview; the apostle tends to see the big picture. This broad frame of reference allows them to know where the church is and see how to move it to where it needs to be. Their desire is to get the job done and they often overlook the details in the process. The glaring weakness of the apostolic gift is that in isolation the person can be perceived as controlling or domineering.

The **prophet** focuses on direction. Their motivation is to hear God, know His will and do it. They want the *now* word and will not be satisfied with anything less. Their perspective is telescopic; what they see they see with great clarity, but they often will not see the periphery. The prophet will focus on one area or issue and will want to know if it is God or not. With prophets there are no gray areas. They want things right, and if it is not, they want to change it now. The weakness of the prophetic ministry in isolation is that they can be intolerant, with little room for others. They also tend to get so invested in what they hear that if their word isn't received, they feel personally rejected.

The **evangelist** is defined by extension, pushing back the darkness and reaching the unreached. Their motivation is to see the lost saved; they want new souls and will do whatever it takes to reach people. Their perspective is wide angle, "Can this be used for the gospel?" If it works, do it. For the evangelist, the end justifies the means as long as souls are saved. Their desire is that none should perish and that every believer should evangelize. Their weakness in isolation is that because of their "whatever it takes" attitude, they can easily slip into error.

The **pastor** is characterized by cohesion. They are motivated to care for the sheep and protect them so they will heal and grow. The pastor's perspective is x-ray vision; they look inside the person and see the heart. They live to see people whole, healed and delivered. They work to clean them up, and hold them together. Their desire is to see people become who they were created to be in God. The weakness of the pastor in isolation is that they can be over-protective of the sheep, holding on to them instead of releasing them as gifts to the wider body.

The **teacher** is all about explanation of the Word. They are motivated by their desire to know and love the Word of God. Their perspective is microscopic; they want to get to the root of why and how it works. The teacher will remain true to the Word and will fight for it to the death. His or her desire is that everyone would have a solid foundation. Their weakness in isolation is that they can easily get bogged down in details and miss the big picture.

If what we have just shared is true, look at the implications as they begin to work together. Apostles will frustrate the pastor because they tend to overlook the individual needs of the sheep in the pursuit of the big goal. And the pastor is afraid the apostle is going to push his people too hard before they are ready. The apostle will never see the details as well as the prophet, which is why they need to work together to fulfill their purpose. The evangelist tries to stir the people up to witness, but the pastor sees the brokenness and wants them healed first. The pastor is leery of the prophet because he is afraid he or she will beat up the sheep, and the prophet sees the pastor as overprotective.

IT CAN GET MESSY!

But as we've said, God never intended any of the ministry gifts to work independent of the others. Each gift should have and maintain close relationships with those who operate in diverse gifts whether they are part of the same local church body or not. The magnificence of God's design is that we all need others. This is crucial because each of the five perspectives is necessary for the body of Christ to come to maturity.

When we know that we are incomplete without others, we begin to value others in a new way. We value our different perspectives and seek to learn from one another's strengths. We will also be careful to cover the weaknesses of others rather than expose them. For this to happen we need to learn the value of diversity and begin to build relationships with other ministries, rather than simply gathering around us gifts that are similar to ours. This paradigm of "unity in diversity" and "interdependent function" can also be applied to racial, cultural, socioeconomic, and even generational divisions in the body.

CHAPTER 6
FELLOWSHIP
OUT OF ISOLATION

I pray that the fellowship of your faith may become effective
PHILEMON 6

In the creation of man God said that it was not good for man to be alone. There were several reasons for this; it did not express the plurality of the Godhead and the need for procreation. But another important reason is that we were created for fellowship, with a desire for social interaction and a need for real connections with others. God designed us with the capacity and the need to form deep and lasting relationships. We are at our best when these life-giving relationships are in place and at our most vulnerable when we are alone.

Notice that the temptation of Jesus took place in isolation in the desert. We are told that Jesus was tempted in the same ways we are tempted. It stands to reason then that His temptation took place in solitude, because that was the place of greatest vulnerability. When we stand together we can take on any adversary, but alone we can become an easy target. When Israel made their exit from Egypt, they were safe as long as they moved together. However, if they lagged behind or got isolated, they became vulnerable to the Amalekites who were just waiting to pick them off (Deut. 25:17).

ISLANDS

The word *isolation* means to be in a place or situation that is separate from others. The word came to English through a Latin word, which means "made into an island." When we isolate ourselves, we become an island unto ourselves. For some this may sound appealing, especially for those of us who like our privacy. The difficulty is not in planning private times in our schedule, but rather when isolation becomes a lifestyle. Not only do we become more vulnerable to the enemy; there are serious health risks to seclusion.

A brief Internet search of the consequences of isolation turns up several disturbing studies. The loneliness that comes with isolation is not just making us sick; it is killing us. Loneliness is a serious health risk. Studies of elderly people and social isolation concluded that those without adequate social interaction were twice as likely to die prematurely. The increased risk is similar to the risk from smoking. And loneliness is about twice as dangerous as obesity. Social isolation also has been found to impair immune function and increase inflammation, which can lead to arthritis, type II diabetes, and even heart disease.

We were created for fellowship as individuals and as leaders in the body of Christ. In fact nowhere in the concept of the church was isolation encouraged. The language used to describe the church calls for a togetherness that is born out of fellowship with one another.

NEW TESTAMENT CHURCH

The primary word used to describe church in the New Testament is *ecclesia*, which means "called out or called forth." The Greeks originally used the word to describe a gathering of citizens called out from their homes into some public place as a political assembly. They would discuss the affairs of the city and make decisions for the citizens. Ecclesia refers to the local structure or government that describes the people who hold the political power and even judicial functions for the good of the city.[5]

FELLOWSHIP OUT OF ISOLATION

When Jesus used the word *ecclesia* to describe the church, He was describing a group of people called out of the world to do the work of the kingdom, a people who responded to His call and agreed to do heaven's work on earth. They served under no other authority than His and as such became His government on earth. As His representatives they had power and authority to exercise the will of the King so that His purposes would be fulfilled. Ecclesia describes the influence that God intended for the church to have in every aspect of society. This idea of the church being the influencers of society got lost in the institutionalizing of church in the third century. Over time the church came under the influence of the very people they were intended to reach.

The second word used to describe the activity of the early church is koinonia, which means "fellowship or communion." It describes the church as a living organism. Koinonia or fellowship describes the family nature of the church as the people of God. The church is where believers come into real life-giving relationships with one another. It is the koinonia that gives life and strength to the ecclesia. The called out ones can influence the society around them because they have real and life-giving fellowship with God and with one another.

DEVOTED TO FELLOWSHIP

Luke wrote in his description of life in the early church that *they were continually devoting themselves to the apostles' teaching and to fellowship, to the breaking of bread and to prayer* (Acts 2:42). **They devoted themselves to fellowship!** Fellowship played a key role in the early church and is just as essential for the church today. It is also an essential discipline for building team ministry. Unfortunately, however, we do not fully grasp the significance of this word in the New Testament, in part, because the English word *fellowship* does not have the same breadth of meaning as the original word *koinonia*.

The English dictionary describes *fellowship* as "the condition of sharing similar interests, ideals, or experiences, the companionship of individuals in a congenial atmosphere and on equal terms." For us fellowship seems more like hanging out with friends and having a good time than a fundamental part of church life. This weak view of fellowship has made it optional in many of our local churches. It has also made it easy to tolerate the clergy/laity divide and has perpetuated non-relational forms of church leadership.

Koinonia includes the idea of fellowship, but it also means "communion, community, communication, contact, distribution, and joint participation." When we *koinonia*, we share in one another's lives; we develop real relationships and we impart things to one another. The root word behind *koinonia* is "partnership;" so when we fellowship with each other, we literally participate in their life. The key idea in the word is that of a partnership, possessing things in common, a belonging in common, or sharing in something. This idea of joint participation carries over into all areas of life, affecting our relationships in a community, a team, an alliance or any joint venture.

FELLOWSHIP ORIGINATES WITH GOD

The idea of fellowship emanates from the heart of God and flows from our relationship with God. It is a manifestation of the nature of the Trinity. Fellowship is the way Father, Son, and Spirit relate to one another; They have been together in relationship from the beginning. The fellowship enjoyed within the Trinity provides part of the very definition of who God is. It also explains why everything He makes is created in relationships and why leadership teams that represent Him must be built on relationship. If we want the church to function as a living organism in the way that God intended, fellowship is a key to keeping us from drifting into dead structure.

When John invited believers to come into fellowship with one another, he indicated that their fellowship originated with the Father and the Son. *What we have seen and heard we proclaim to you also, that you also may have fellowship with us; and indeed our fellowship is with the Father, and with His Son Jesus Christ* (1 John 1:3). True fellowship is restored because the blood of Jesus has made the way for us to come back into fellowship with the Father. His death and resurrection removed the barrier, making genuine fellowship possible. Once our intimacy with the Father and the Son is reestablished, we have the working model of the kind of fellowship we are to engage in with each other. This new model of fellowship begins with the restoration of Fatherhood.

FELLOWSHIP WITH THE FATHER

The idea of fatherhood came under attack in the third century as the church moved from living organism to organization. Father became an ecclesiastical title instead of a living relationship. As we seek to return to the body of Christ being a living organism, we must recapture the function of spiritual fathers and mothers in the church. A couple of years ago I did a survey among the young people in our church. One of the questions I asked was their perception of the greatest need for their generation. They overwhelmingly highlighted the need for spiritual fathers and mothers to be an active part of their lives.

We live in a fatherless generation in desperate need of true fathering. Many try to fill this void in human relationships without first coming into relationship with their heavenly Father. Without this vital relationship with God our Father, earthly relationships we build will always drift off balance, because without the relationship with our heavenly Father, we are asking people to fill a void that only God can fill. We need spiritual fathers and mothers in the faith, but they cannot fill the role of our heavenly Father.

Earthly relationships will always disappoint at some point. They mess up, they change their mind and appear inconsistent, but our Father God will never disappoint. He models perfect fathering. Never in competition, He remains faithful and never abandons His children. He has no favorites but loves each one of His children unconditionally. As someone has said, He is too loving to be unkind, and too wise to make mistakes.

FELLOWSHIP WITH THE SON

Fellowship with the Son is equally as important as fellowship with the Father. The Son is the exact representation of the Father; if you have seen the Son, you have seen the Father. Jesus came to reveal the Father and lived his life demonstrating the nature and character of the Father. Jesus is how the Father chose to reveal Himself to the world. There is no restored fellowship with the Father without the sacrifice of the Son. But it does not stop there; the fellowship with the Son is a life-long pursuit of His presence. So, we have fellowship with the Father but we also have fellowship with the Son - first as the Lamb of God who took away the sin of the world, then as the model of life lived as a man full of the Holy Spirit, then as the Risen King, the Lion of the tribe of Judah, then as our great intercessor. Jesus is the center of our life and the passion of our whole existence. As we glory in the acceptance we have received from the Father and the wonder of our empowering by the Spirit, let us not forget to develop a passion for Jesus.

Our spiritual father, Philip Mohabir, always asked us the same question when we would meet with him. "Is your fellowship with Jesus still sweet? Has anything stolen your passion for Him?" He was so in love with Jesus that it showed through every aspect of his life. When he preached, as soon as he began to talk about Jesus, he would begin to weep, and any time he mentioned the blood, his voice would drop to a reverent hush. He knew the power of the blood and would never let us forget that the central relationship we are to maintain as believers is a deep, passionate love for Jesus.

FELLOWSHIP WITH THE HOLY SPIRIT

The fellowship that we have with the Father and with one another is sustained by fellowship with the Holy Spirit. *Therefore if there is any ... fellowship of the Spirit...* (Phil. 2:1). Regular fellowship with the Holy Spirit will sustain our fellowship with one another. It is inconceivable that we can maintain correct relationships without first being in right relationship with God. The Holy Spirit reminds us of the work of the cross in restoring relationships and causes us to remember the responsibility of maintaining our human relationships. The next verse tells us that the result of our fellowship with the Spirit is unity with other believers, *then make my joy complete by being … united in spirit, intent on one purpose* (Phil. 2:2). The Spirit unifies!

The encouragement we receive from Christ, the love we receive from the Father, and the fellowship of the Holy Spirit produce in us true *koinonia* with one another, allowing us to come into a unity of purpose. Our *koinonia* with each other is based on our *koinonia* with the Father, Son, and Holy Spirit. The fellowship the Trinity enjoys creates a hunger in us to know true fellowship with one another.

FELLOWSHIP WITH ONE ANOTHER

Because of this ongoing relationship with all three Persons of the Trinity, Christians have fellowship with one another. *But if we walk in the Light as He Himself is in the Light, we have fellowship with one another, and the blood of Jesus His Son cleanses us from all sin* (1 John 1:7). The relationship we maintain with each other comes as a direct reflection of the depth of our fellowship and intimacy with God. We lie to ourselves if we think that we can walk in the light of His presence and not maintain a corresponding fellowship with others.

When we walk in the light in our relationship with God, two profound transformations take place. First, we have real fellowship with one another, and second, the blood cleanses us from all sin. So, we can walk clean before God and before our brothers and sisters. Notice that the cleansing work of the blood in this verse appears to be a consequence of maintaining correct relationships with others. The gospel of reconciliation, first and foremost, restored our relationship with God. But of equal importance in God's eyes is that we learn to walk in restored fellowship with one another as a direct reflection of our newfound relationship with Him. We must learn the meaning of fellowship with our brothers and sisters.

Earlier in the chapter we gave a brief definition to the Greek word *koinonia*, but it has such a rich word meaning that it deserves more attention. *Koinonia* is a derivative of "*koinos*," the word for "common." Most dictionaries give definitions that fall into at least three broad categories. Because this concept is so central to building community and to establishing team leadership, we want to closely examine these three categories, which are participation, impartation, and communion.

PARTICIPATION

In Greek, *koinonia* implies the idea of an association, a common effort, or a partnership. This is consistent with the meaning of our English word *participation*, defined as "the act of taking part in something." Participation comes from a Latin root word, which means, "to become a partner." So when we fellowship with someone, we become a partner with them. When we fellowship in the body of Christ, we are joined together and aligned in relationship. *Koinonia* suggests a powerful common interest that has the capacity to hold people together.

The strength of this bond of partnership is further demonstrated by the use of *koinonia* in Greek marriage contracts where the husband and wife are asked to agree to a joint-participation in the necessities of life.

When *koinonia* is applied to our spiritual relationship, it unites us in our common experiences, interests, and goals. This partnership in the faith creates a bond of fellowship, which allows us to share in one another's joy, as well as in their pain. This kind of true fellowship breaks down isolationism and fulfills the human need for belonging and companionship. *Koinonia* is by nature loving, sharing, caring, and generous because it originates in the heart of the Father.

This partnership aspect of fellowship has purpose, meaning that true fellowship is never passive but active. When we fellowship with one another, it is not about what we can receive as much as it is about how much we can give. Whenever we see the idea of *koinonia* it is linked to action; so, it is not just about being together but also about doing together. When we fellowship we look for opportunities to bless one another and to bless those outside our circle of fellowship. This active aspect of *koinonia* is directly linked to the growth of our faith.

Paul links our fellowship with our faith when he wrote, *I pray that the fellowship of your faith may become effective through the knowledge of every good thing which is in you for Christ's sake* (Philem. 6). Faith is not passive; it grows in the context of the community of believers. **So faith needs fellowship in order to grow and develop**. When faith and fellowship unite, the work of the ministry becomes more effective. As we come to know the good things that are in one another and share them, the testimony stirs us to action. Our fellowship is a fellowship of faith and as such it should increase and grow our faith.

Fellowship is such a powerful word, however, that we must guard the things we fellowship with. Paul warned the church, *do not be bound together with unbelievers; for what partnership have righteousness and lawlessness, or what fellowship has light with darkness* (2 Cor. 6:14). What are we partnering with? If we hang out with people who are always negative or critical, we may find ourselves repeating the same things. If we partner with the wrong attitudes, we limit the effectiveness of our call. **Relationships without a spiritual foundation always cause us to participate with the wrong things!**

Because fellowship is a partnership, it builds close relationship. When we are in fellowship, we grow as we embrace the thoughts and ideas of those we spend time with. The heart of fellowship requires open and frank communication. When we open our hearts what comes out? Are we communicating words of life or words of death? We are either building people up or tearing them down. So ask yourself, what does light have in common with darkness? What part should gossip, backbiting, or any other kind of sin have in our fellowship?

IMPARTATION

The second aspect of *koinonia* is that of *impartation*. The Greek word means to have a share in a thing or to be a sharer. The idea can be that the things we hold in common we share in, but it can also mean to share what we have with another. This second meaning coincides more with the sense of our English word *impartation*. It comes from *impart* which means to communicate information, to give or bestow something. The root comes from two Latin words *im* meaning in or into and *partre* meaning to divide, so when combined it means to divide with another or to have a share in something. When we impart we gladly give others a share in or a part of what we have. When we lay hands on a person to pray for them, we are literally fellowshipping with them; we are giving them a share in what we have.

Paul tells the church that because of their love, *we were well-pleased to impart to you not only the gospel of God but also our own lives…* (1 Thess. 2:8). We impart more than just the message; we also impart the messenger – ourselves. We cannot fellowship at arm's length, because fellowship costs something. God has created us with the ability to give into or share with others what God has given us. *Koinonia* therefore implies a spirit of generous sharing or the act of giving. Impartation is an unselfish releasing of all that the Spirit of God has bestowed on us in hopes that the other person will get even more than we received.

Impartation also means that we will be impacted by those we fellowship with. We are influenced by fellowship and by the relationships that we develop. Whatever you join yourself to will impact you! This is not a response of fear but a walk of wisdom. We are not to fear relationships with the world, but **we must guard where we let our hearts be joined.** The Spirit of God in us is much greater than the spirit that is in the world. Under the old covenant if we touched an unclean person, we became unclean, but in the New Covenant when we touch someone who is unclean, they receive an impartation from us.

COMMUNION

The third category is *communion*. Communion begins with the idea of community that denotes a "common unity" of purpose and interests. It includes friendship, relationship, companionship, and finally communion, which is an intimate sharing that comes out of having life in common. So, fellowship in the body of Christ is sharing with one another the life we have in common.

FELLOWSHIP OUT OF ISOLATION

As Christians we participate in salvation both individually and corporately. Individually, we receive the new life in Christ and then are placed in the body of Christ in which we participate with one another in all the benefits of this new life. Thus, our fellowship with others provides a true reflection of our relationship with God.

When Paul is dealing with division in the church, he uses the Lord's Supper to teach our joint responsibility. *Is not the cup of blessing which we bless a sharing in the blood of Christ? Is not the bread which we break a sharing in the body of Christ?* (1 Cor. 10:16) Both the bread and the cup are something we share. They serve as an indication of our joint-participation, the things we have in common, in the body and blood of Christ. We participate in common with one another in the salvation benefits that proceed from the shed blood and the broken body of the Lord Jesus.

The act of Communion celebrates what Jesus did for us and requires that we examine ourselves before we take it. Generally, we apply this to sin in our lives and while true, it is only one aspect. The context of this injunction is fellowship, our communion with one another. When we break bread together, one aspect of this ordinance celebrates our relationship with our brothers and sisters in Christ. Paul goes on to say that, *For he who eats and drinks, eats and drinks judgment to himself if he does not judge the body rightly. For this reason many among you are weak and sick, and a number sleep* (1 Cor. 11:29, 30). This is one of the only passages of scripture that tells us why Christians get sick. If we do not judge the body rightly, in other words, if we do not maintain correct fellowship within the body, there are consequences. This violation of fellowship has caused Christians to be sick. So, before we take communion we would suggest the need to get our relationships right; it is the same principle as getting relationships right before we give an offering.

Koinonia builds a bond of love and trust that overcomes our fears and insecurities. It creates a safe atmosphere where people are valued and brought into wholeness. When fellowship flows from the Spirit, it heals divisions and mends brokenness. The church becomes a community, which resembles family. In this environment we work together for a single purpose - to lift Jesus up together!

Fellowship provides the context for the fulfillment of Jesus' prayer, that they may all be one; even as You, Father, are in Me and I in You, *that they also may be in Us, so that the world may believe that You sent Me* (John 17:21). Christ prayed that His people might have the kind of fellowship with one another that He had with the Father. He also pointed out that this kind of fellowship is essential for the world to know the truth. Fellowship with God and with one another is essential to fruitfulness in this harvest season.

CHAPTER 7
RELATIONSHIPS
SUSTAINED BY THE SPIRIT

For by one Spirit we were all baptized into one body
1 CORINTHIANS 12:13

During my sophomore year of college the engineering department bought a computer. They stuck it in our old dining hall, and the single monster took up most of the space. It was a wonder to see and we eagerly watched as it whirred to life. Programming and data entry required punch cards meticulously prepared with the appropriate information. Then our stack of cards went into the machine, and after a few minutes of noisy deliberation, out came the solution. That same year Neil Armstrong and Buzz Aldrin landed on the moon!

The next semester the college added a keyboard to the machine. Of course, only the instructor was allowed to use it. We still did our work with stacks of cards, and I think my final project for fluid mechanics was a stack almost a foot tall. Little did we know the impact this technology would have on us. The onset of this cumbersome machine would transform the way we communicate.

CONNECTIONS
Years later the computer makes vast resources of information available almost instantaneously. Hours spent in research have been reduced to minutes with

more and more resources at our fingertips. The phones we carry get more sophisticated each year, making communication faster and easier, allowing us to stay in touch with more people. Social media has helped reestablish connections to school classmates and long forgotten friends. But all the discovery and reconnection does not necessarily produce meaningful relationships; that requires more than a Facebook conversation. While technology does connect us to more people, it isn't the final answer for isolation. Unfortunately, all the contacts just seem to spread thin the little time we have and make many of our relationships disturbingly shallow.

We feel more connected through social media and online networking and yet in many ways we are more disconnected than ever. Today's technologies make communication faster but not necessarily better. Texting and tweeting may help us stay in touch, but a genuine relationship requires personal contact. Relationships require time getting to know one another, developing trust and becoming aware of each other's strengths and weaknesses. However, for most of us, time is in short supply and the building and maintaining of real relationships falls dangerously near the bottom of our priorities.

Recently I was asked to work with a pastor who had experienced some difficulties in his personal life and consequently in his church. I had known this brother for many years, and if asked, would have said that we were friends. However, in the busyness of life we had spent little time together. In our first meeting he and his wife made the statement that they had no friends. The admission startled me, saddened me and caused me to later examine my own relational priorities. How can we be in ministry for years and believe in the value of relationships, and yet let ourselves get in the position where we have no true friends - a place so isolated that we have no real relationships, no one we can be honest with, and no one to stand with us in difficult times?

The lack of relationship made the task of bringing restoration extremely difficult. Without the bridge of relational trust, it proved almost impossible to bring meaningful input to the leader. In fact, as is often the case, the lack of relationship meant that any attempt we made to bring correction to his behavior had the tendency to push him away, damaging our relationship bridge even further.

So how do we avoid the pitfalls of isolation? How do we maintain meaningful relationships that have real accountability? How do we learn to work together as a team in the way God designed?

We have already seen the necessity of understanding our desperate need for one another. We have also seen that without one another we can never fulfill our calling. We have realized that when functioning in isolation, none of us ever fully represents Christ. But there is a Person that brings the pieces together. We must come to understand that *leadership teams in the Body of Christ form and function as a work of the Holy Spirit.* Until Pentecost the disciples had seen team modeled and they had participated as pairs; but when the Spirit fell, they found themselves galvanized into the team God designed with the capacity to change the world.

THE HOLY SPIRIT AND TEAM

Obedience to Jesus' command brought them together in the upper room and created the atmosphere for the Holy Spirit to fall. Scripture tells us *…they were all together in one place* (Acts 2:1). The word *together* means "in one accord." This definition may not at first glance appear to be life changing, but in this case the antonyms of the word reveal more than the definition. Webster lists the antonyms for *together* as: "separately, one's own, private, alone, by oneself." **The opposite of together is the very thing God warned us about in creation.** Operating alone in ministry is the antithesis to the plan and purpose of God for our lives. As leaders we must heed the warning and determine to resist the drift toward isolation that so easily takes place in our religious culture.

Learning to work together is an integral part of God's design, not just for creating a loving atmosphere, but as an essential environment for mission. The transformation at Pentecost provided the first fulfillment of Jesus' prayer. He prayed that His disciples would be perfected in unity (John 17:23). As a result of this perfected unity, the world would come to know Jesus. The disciples, united as a team and emboldened by the Spirit, came out of the upper room displaying the multifaceted glory of God to the world.

SEALED BY THE SPIRIT

Sally and I have had many relationships that have fed into our lives over the course of our ministry. But from the moment we received the baptism in the Holy Spirit, we began to find new depth of relational fellowship. The Holy Spirit who sealed us (2 Cor. 1:22) had not only marked us as belonging to Him, He changed the way we related to others. Almost immediately, real relationships began to develop around the common sharing of the Spirit and a desire to know more of His power and presence. In the same way that we had experienced a new hunger for the Word, we discovered a deep longing for real lasting relationships that would stand the test of adversity. We began to see the people God had placed around us in a new way.

No longer did we focus on their flaws but on the glory of the work of Jesus in and through the lives of each individual. We began to see people through the lens of grace, which allowed us to live relationally with mercy and not judgment. The Holy Spirit opened our eyes to see people through His perspective of expectancy. We began to trust the life of God in others, believing the best about them even when they failed. This hope-filled way of living allowed us to go deep in relationships without fear of rejection. Paul's revelation of the glory present in the ministry of the Spirit (2 Cor. 3:8) took on fresh meaning. We began to see that every aspect of life flows from fellowship with the Holy Spirit. Real Spirit-birthed relationships with our brothers and sisters release the glory of God into our midst!

THE LIFE OF THE SPIRIT

In creation the Holy Spirit breathed life into dust, giving us life from His breath. Job picked up this theme when he said that, *The Spirit of God has made me, and the breath of the Almighty gives me life* (Job 33:4). The Holy Spirit breathes life into the body and He remains to sustain that life. The same life of the Spirit works to bring all the individual parts of the body into connection and unity with each other.

Ezekiel sees this in his vision and prophesies that the Lord will put His Spirit, *within you, and you will come to life…* (Ezek. 37:14). His word comes in the context of the valley of dry bones; the various parts of the body came to life, found each other and came together. There is a natural fulfillment in Israel with their return to the land, but there is a spiritual fulfillment in the church as well, which brings us into the kind of orchestrated oneness that God designed for us to live in. The Holy Spirit today works to bring the individual parts of the body together if we will allow Him room to move us. He will guide us to find one another and bring us into proper alignment. He then works to sustain the divine connections that He arranges.

John writes that, *It is the Spirit who gives life* (John 6:63). The life flow in the church begins with an individual fellowship with the Spirit that overflows into the corporate body through our connections with others. The Spirit of God indwells the body (1 Cor. 6:19), and this applies both individually and corporately. We belong to Him; we are His body, the dwelling place of the Holy Spirit who lives in us and gives us life. This applies to every area of our life, including leadership in the body.

SPIRIT-LED LEADERSHIP

It is the life of the Spirit that establishes and sustains leadership. Scripture tells us that as leaders we are to, *be on guard for yourselves and for all the flock, among which the Holy Spirit has made you overseers…* (Acts 20:28). The call to leadership comes as a work of the Holy Spirit. The Spirit places us in position wherever

He desires and keeps us secure in that position. We see this in action when the disciples began to expand the leadership by introducing deacons. They were told by the Spirit to choose those with *…good reputation, full of the Spirit and of wisdom* (Acts 6:3).

Leadership was first to be measured by the fullness of the Holy Spirit. Leadership based on giftedness or rational thinking alone cannot build a leadership team. When the disciples received the outpouring of the Holy Spirit in Jerusalem, they received more than power for ministry. They also received the life or presence of the Spirit for ministry. After Saul's conversion Ananias told Saul he was sent to him *so that you may regain your sight and be filled with the Holy Spirit* (Acts 9:17). Holy Spirit transitioned Saul to Paul and anointed him for his calling and ministry.

As Gentiles were added into the church the cultural issues threatened to tear the early church apart, but the work of the Spirit kept it together. Peter testified that as he began to speak to them, *the Holy Spirit fell upon them just as He did upon us at the beginning* (Acts 11:15). The Holy Spirit marked the Gentiles as belonging; the Spirit was the seal of God's approval and for the disciples that proved sufficient evidence.

The work of the Holy Spirit in a leadership team does not stop with the seal of unity; He also works within the team to give the direction necessary to fulfill the task. Remember in Antioch, the leadership was worshiping and praying when the Spirit spoke into their midst. *Set apart for Me Barnabas and Saul for the work to which I have called them* (Acts 13:2). The Holy Spirit spoke and the leadership team responded. Once they had heard the Spirit, they stood as one in the decision.

THE SPIRIT UNITES

Paul told the Ephesians that they had to be *diligent to preserve the unity of the Spirit in the bond of peace* (Eph. 4:3). Unity is first *of* the Spirit and is preserved as each individual remains *in* the Spirit. Team ministry operates from a place of unity dependent on the work of the Spirit. This means that unity in a team can prove illusive, especially when the team is comprised of very diverse gifts. So maintaining unity takes consistent communion with the Holy Spirit.

The Greek word *preserve* from the verse above has several meanings, including "to guard from loss or injury or to prevent from escaping." For teams to sustain on a long-term basis, intimacy with the Spirit must be a high value. Paul reminds us that, *there is one body and one Spirit, just as also you were called in one hope of your calling* (Eph. 4:4). It is the Spirit that marks us as one. This means that there can be no true unity outside of the Spirit.

The lowest common denominator unity that many seek fails to unite, because only the Spirit baptizes us into one. Many citywide prayer groups work for unity, but all too often the unspoken rule is that Pentecostals and Charismatics must leave the gifts of the Holy Spirit at the door. But this fear of causing offense effectively removes or at the very least limits the work of the unifying Person.

Paul tells the Corinthians who struggled to maintain unity that by one *Spirit we were all baptized into one body, whether Jews or Greeks, whether slaves or free, and we were all made to drink of one Spirit* (1 Cor. 12:13). The cross destroyed all divisions and released the power and presence of the Spirit to function as a bridge of reconciliation. To the Philippian believers Paul describes the personal walk and disciplines that produce life in the corporate context. The first verse challenges the individual, *if there is any fellowship with the Spirit…* (Phil.2:1). Corporate unity will prove illusive unless each individual maintains personal intimacy with the Spirit. Paul then goes on in the next verse to describe the outcome, *then make my joy complete… by being united in Spirit…* (Phil. 2:2). Look at this! If we would all consistently fellowship with the Spirit, then corporately as we come together, we would experience a unity of the Spirit. There is a direct connection.

So the unity of the Spirit is not found in agreement on every point of doctrine but in a common fellowship with the Holy Spirit and with each other. When the

Holy Spirit fills the believer, part of His task is to reveal Jesus. The extent of our individual connection to the Head, Jesus, provides an accurate measure of our potential to walk in unity with our brothers and sisters. The perfect oneness in the Godhead will be revealed and imparted through this ongoing fellowship. So, the more we allow the Holy Spirit to reveal Jesus to us, the more we will function together as a team.

In John 17:23 Jesus speaks of "being perfected in unity;" this phrase can also be translated "being perfected into a unit," which we will discuss in detail later, but let's apply it to team. A unit serves as a group of individuals coming together to accomplish a task. We could use the word to describe a highly trained and unified sports team. A unit always unifies around purpose; members are trained and disciplined to respond immediately with their objective in mind. They learn one another's strengths and weaknesses and understand how to react in any given situation. This is true team ministry, recognizing that we desperately need each other and understanding that only together are we complete.

To function as a unit we need the revelation that no matter how gifted we are, without the Holy Spirit, team will not function. The Spirit breathes life into us as a team; the Spirit unites us as a team; the Spirit empowers us as a team and the Holy Spirit sustains the life of the team. The revelation that we are incomplete by God's design in and of itself is powerless to change us. However, if we will surrender to the unifying power of the Holy Spirit, He will work to join us to the right people and then work in us to maintain that joint. This dynamic work of the Spirit completes us by placing us in team with others so that together the world can see a more complete image of our precious Lord Jesus.

REVIVAL LEADERSHIP

In our study of revivals, one of the key features that set Toronto apart was that they set out to be Spirit-led and resisted being personality driven. John and Carol Arnott from the Airport Vineyard had received a powerful impartation from Claudio Freidzon but at that point had not yet seen a significant move of God in their church. From that place of hunger, they invited Randy Clark to come and do four nights of meetings. They had heard what God was doing in the church Randy pastored in Saint Louis and were hungry for the same kind of breakthrough.

The first night January 20, 1994, the Holy Spirit fell on 120 people and this quickly and dramatically grew over the next few weeks. Within days the 400 seat capacity was full and they added an overflow, seating 300 more. Lives were powerfully transformed as the power of God came to heal, deliver and restore. The outpouring became known as "The Father's Blessing."

As with all revivals in history there were many manifestations of the Holy Spirit mixed with a little flesh. Although these manifestations became the lightning rod for criticism, there remained a powerful transferable anointing released that changed lives forever. The leadership walked the difficult balance of honoring the life of the Spirit and refusing to let order quench the life. It would have been easier to do what others had done and bring "order," but the leadership made the courageous choice to follow the Spirit and not their critics.

Over the months the meetings grew until, "by the end of 1995, 600,000 people had visited Toronto from almost every nation on the planet." In addition, there were over 900 first time conversions in the renewal's first year[6] and 20 years later its worldwide impact continues to expand.

While the growth in the locality was exciting, the most profound effect has been the continued and increasing global momentum. Across the earth there are churches and ministries that would acknowledge that their effective ministry traces back to the impartation they received in Toronto. The renewal jumped to England when the Spirit fell in Holy Trinity Brompton and then spread out to literally thousands of denominational churches. Another early visitor to the revival was Nicky Gumbel from Holy Trinity, who became leader of the Alpha Course. The Guardian newspaper reported in 2000 that "a quarter of a million agnostics have found God through Gumbel." And in the same article they quoted Gumbel as saying that "the Toronto Blessing was the kick-start Alpha needed."[7]

Bethel Church Redding, California traces at least part of their revival culture to the empowering they received at Toronto. And three ministries, Heidi and Rolland Baker in Mozambique, Leif Hetland in Pakistan and Henry Madava from Ukraine, who were touched by this awakening, have each seen over a million souls come to Christ as a result of the impartation they received.

So why is Toronto still continuing after 20 years? Why has it had the global impact that qualifies it as a genuine awakening? Why do we believe that this is a working model of a stream of revival that never ends? One key piece is that they worked as a team!

TEAM MINISTRY

In the beginning the meetings were extended day by day, but the leadership team soon realized that they needed a plan. Initially, they discussed plans for another 30 days and then began to ask the question: What happens if this move goes on for another year? The answer to their question is now history and decisions made early on in the meetings laid a foundation, which allowed this revival to continue to grow.

John and Carol functioned in the Apostolic and Pastoral role in the revival and Randy operated as the evangelist, spending 42 of the first 60 days in Toronto. Early on John felt the need to build a team who could help manage and sustain what God was doing. He added in the prophetic with Wes Campbell, Larry Randolph, and Mark DuPont joining the leadership team. God in His wisdom had found someone willing to do it His way. His way was to build a team that could sustain the move of God and carry it forward to future generations.

From the beginning the team dynamic kept the outpouring from being about a single personality and let it focus on hosting the presence of God. In fact, early on in the renewal neither John nor Randy were at the meetings for one week, and even without them, the revival continued unabated. Their prayer that it would be about the Holy Spirit and not about them was answered.

With crowds at capacity, John and Randy looked for ways to spread the revival. When they would notice a group of people from one church coming to the meetings together, they would offer to go out to those churches. Often the revival would break out in the new venue. This decision to spread the fire meant that at one point there were as many as seven churches experiencing the outpouring at the same time.

In the end Toronto was not about the Arnotts or Randy Clark; it was not about the personalities that preached. In fact as John began to move out more, pastors who had been touched in the revival were given the opportunity to preach. Toronto was about a group of hungry people who went to the trouble to create an environment **to host the presence of God**. It was about a leadership so sensitive to the Holy Spirit that they built a team of leaders to carry the load.

From this same understanding of the nature of revival, several of the ministries touched by the outpouring formed the Revival Alliance. This team includes John and Carol Arnott, Bill and Benni Johnson, Randy and DeAnne Clark, Georgian and Winnie Banov, Che and Sue Ahn, and Rolland and Heidi Baker. These global charismatic leaders continue to walk together as an apostolic company, each with their own strengths but together for the sake of the kingdom.

PART II
PRINCIPLES FOR IMPLEMENTING TEAM MINISTRY

God has given each of you a gift
from his great variety of spiritual gifts
Use them well to serve one another.
ROMANS 12:5 NLT

CHAPTER 8
AGREEMENT
JUST ADD GRACE

Can two people walk together without agreeing on the direction?
AMOS 3:3 NLT

God instituted the concept of agreement; we see this in marriage, in family, in church and even in society. Without agreement society as we know it would cease to function. There would be no families, no businesses and no sports teams. In fact most of the things we enjoy require some kind of agreement. Without agreement people would live in isolation, never realizing their full potential, because **there can be no success without the power of agreement.**

In the creation of mankind the power of agreement is present in the decision, *let us make man in our image*. Father, Son and Spirit were in agreement that man should be created in Their image. Even though man was created first as an individual, this was amended with the creation of Eve so that the agreement, which was expressed in the Godhead, would be superimposed into the dynamic of the family. Without male coming into agreement with female there would be no children and no fulfillment to the command to be fruitful and multiply. Actually, everything God requires of humanity (reigning, reproducing, reconciling) involves coming into agreement with someone else.

INCOMPLETE BY DESIGN

The English word *agreement* has several meanings, each of which lend something to our understanding. The basic definition is "a harmony of opinion, action or character." In spiritual terms this means that to be in <u>harmony of opinion</u> requires a meeting of the minds so that opinions flow from a mutual submission to the mind of Christ. <u>Harmony of action</u> requires that we unify our effort for the good of others and not simply to serve our individual demands. <u>Harmony of character</u> requires a focus on developing Christ-like character individually, which will ultimately draw us into agreement.

The English language has borrowed words from several European languages and various shades of meaning come with them. The French root to the word *agreement* is "*agreer*" which means "to please." The idea behind the word is to receive someone with favor or to take pleasure in those in whom we find agreement. True relationships are a pleasure. These friendships are the kind in which we do not have to hold a guard up; we can be ourselves. We can let our hair down, be at ease and not worry about what others are thinking. Whether we admit it or not, we all need these kinds of relationships.

The Hebrew word for *agreement* gives more insight into the power of this concept. In Amos 3:3 the prophet makes the declaration *"how can two walk together unless they be agreed."* Agreement is a prerequisite for life or ministry together. The word used here *ya`ad* means "to fix upon, to meet, to summon, to engage or betroth, to assemble in one accord."

There are two key elements in this verse. First, in order to walk in agreement we must make an agreement. Agreement does not just happen; it is something you have to work at; it takes effort. If you decide to buy something, you do not have anything until you make a deal. In the natural, both buyer and seller have to give a little for both to come into agreement. If one side will not give in, then we must decide, "Can we live without this?" If we cannot, then make the agreement on their terms.

AGREEMENT: JUST ADD GRACE

Second, making agreement means agreement on a common purpose and direction. We must have a purpose if we are to walk together. The word *agreement* used in Exodus 21:8 is translated "betrothal" - two people who have made a commitment to walk together into marriage. Agreement then expresses the idea of a strong relationship with a commitment to go deeper. Once an agreement is reached, it expresses a decision to stay together even if it gets rough. This kind of commitment in the body of Christ will produce something in the Kingdom, because it is built with fruitfulness in mind.

CREATED FOR FELLOWSHIP

In the Garden of Eden man and woman were created to have perfect fellowship with God. Each day they spent time together. There was perfect agreement, because they were in His image. Man and woman thought like Him and acted like Him. But the free will, which was inherited as a part of the image of the Creator, became the doorway through which sin and separation came in. Through the fall, they lost agreement with the Creator. Separation, shame and condemnation then flooded the relationship. Mankind in their fallen condition could no longer come into agreement with a holy God.

Long before the fall, God had already made a way for us to come back into agreement with Him. In the design of the tabernacle in the wilderness God gave a pattern for restored agreement between God and man. In the instructions to build the Ark of the Covenant we see the new pattern for agreement. Moses was told to build the Ark that would contain the tablets of the law, then over the Ark as a cover he was to build a mercy seat. This is where the blood of the sacrifice would be sprinkled once per year by the high priest. Then God made a statement of profound significance *There I will meet with you; and from above the mercy seat… I will speak to you about all that I will give you in commandment for the sons of Israel* (Exod. 25:22).

God says that He was creating a place where He could meet with Moses, a place where they could talk and fellowship, a place where Moses could receive instructions for leading the people. The word *meet* used here is more than just a meeting; it is the same word used for agreement. Over the mercy seat God could and would come into agreement with Moses. The blood on the mercy seat literally covered the tablets of the law, which were kept just below it in the ark. The blood allowed God to view Moses prophetically through the finished work of Christ. The righteousness of the Son could now be applied to Moses. We, who were separated from God by sin, could now come back into agreement because of the blood on the mercy seat.

Run to the mercy seat! God has provided a place of meeting for us. It is not found in self-effort, making ourselves good enough, becoming strong enough, or trying to be spiritual enough. It is found in His mercy and grace! We can never do enough to win His favor; so, let us stop and accept His grace freely given to us. Not only is grace the only access to restored relationship with God, it comes in an unlimited supply. **No situation or relationship can ever be beyond His grace!**

God has made the way for us and now we must choose to come back into relationship with Him through the blood of the Son. He has made agreement available; now all that remains is for us to agree with Him. Run to the mercy seat and agreement with God will be restored. Run to the mercy seat and past failures will no longer hold power over us. Run to the mercy seat and our identity will be changed. Run to the mercy seat and find the grace to trust again.

The word of God says that *If God is for us, who is against us?* (Rom. 8:31). Agreement with God is more powerful than the whole world against us. When we come into agreement with God in His way, we allow Him to work on our behalf. In agreement with Him we become partners in ministry. Everything He asks us to do, He partners with us and provides the people, the anointing and the resources to accomplish the task. This extends to every arena of life.

However, running to the mercy seat is also the way we walk in agreement with others. The gospel demands that I relate to others over the blood on the mercy seat. When I look at my brother, I need to see him as God sees him through the finished work of the cross. I can be in full agreement with the Christ that I see in my brother or sister even with my faults and theirs. What a sad state we would be in if we could not fellowship with the Father until all our stuff was dealt with. The same is true in the body of Christ.

This kind of agreement stops division in the body of Christ. *Now I exhort you, brethren, by the name of our Lord Jesus Christ, that you all agree and that there be no divisions among you, but that you be made complete in the same mind and in the same judgment* (1 Cor. 1:10). The word agree here means "to speak the same thing." Coming into agreement over the mercy seat is the antidote to divisions. Only when we are in agreement are we made complete, in the same mind, and in the same judgment.

The word *complete* used here has three distinct meanings. First, it means, "to repair what has been broken." When we come into agreement, anything broken is put back together. **This is the healing power of agreement**. Second, the word means "to adjust, to fit, to put in order, and to arrange." When we come into agreement, we find our place. The interaction with our brothers and sisters causes us to fit together into a team and become more effective than we could have ever been on our own. A worship team with division in the ranks will struggle to bring others into the presence of God. But when they are in right relationship, the anointing increases. Finally, the word *complete* means "to perfect, or bring to a finished state." God's design for us is to walk in agreement with those He places us in relationship with in such a way that we complete and complement one another so that together we grow to maturity.

PART OF A SYMPHONY

The Greek word for *agree* used in 1 Corinthians 1:10 is *sumfooneoo*. It means "to sound together, or to be in accord," and it comes from the root word for harmony. We get our English word symphony from this Greek root. Think about a symphony for a moment; it is an amazing object lesson on agreement. An orchestra is made up of dozens of instruments, some naturally tuned to different keys. In front of them are sheets of music representing the different parts they are to perform. Each musician has practiced and become proficient on their instrument and each knows the part they are to play in the musical selection. Few of them will ever do solo work, because the sounds they make and the parts they play were created to blend with others.

The sound during the tuning process can seem discordant as each instrument is brought into pitch. Then, at the appointed time, the conductor taps his podium and all is quiet. With one motion of the baton the individual instruments become one voice. *Forgotten are the idiosyncrasies of each individual, now there is only one voice, one sound releasing harmony.*

One of the meanings of the Hebrew word agree is "destination." Two people who do not have the same goals can never be in full agreement. They will always end up pulling in different directions, because in fact their destinations are different. Imagine again the orchestra; only this time someone has shuffled the sheet music. Now, instead of the instruments being in harmony, they are all on a different page and confusion reigns. They will never get back together unless they go back to playing the same music.

When both parties agree on a destination, agreement flows naturally into the relationship. My wife and I have counseled many couples that were in difficulty; most of the time there is a lack of unity on the direction for their lives. These are the ones that are hard to help, because if they cannot agree on a destination, it is unlikely that they will have the resolve to work through the issues they face.

AGREEMENT ATTRACTS THE PRESENCE

Another powerful result of agreement is that it ushers in both the ***promise*** and the ***presence*** of God. Matthew writes, *Again I say to you, that if two of you agree on earth about anything that they may ask, it shall be done for them by My Father who is in heaven* (Matt. 18:19). God puts a very high value on agreement.

AGREEMENT: JUST ADD GRACE

His promise is that when we walk together, **He responds by answering prayers that seem impossible**. Agreement is God's law for accomplishing His purpose and because it is His law, it will produce fruitfulness in any arena. If you are struggling to get answers from heaven, check your relationships and come into agreement. Heaven will respond with abundance.

I remember the day we made the decision to go to the mission field. I had graduated from college and Sally and I planned to work for a year to get our school debt paid off before going to Africa. At the end of the year we had added our first child, Rachel, and after a year of working we had made no headway on the debt. We sat together one evening and realized that if something did not change, we would never get there. So we came into agreement that despite the debt we would enroll in the next mission candidate school and trust God with the debt. The next morning I called up Africa Inland Mission and enrolled us in the school that was just three months away.

That same evening we got a phone call from a lady that we had met only once. Her opening question was, "What is keeping you from the mission field?" I explained to her what we had done the night before and told her that the delay was the school loans I had to pay back before we would be allowed to go to the field. She asked me to give her the total debt we owed and as soon as I did, she wrote out a check for the entire amount! We got the check in the mail a few days later. The agreement that Sally and I made had unlocked a supernatural provision that propelled us into our destiny.

But agreement is more than just increase in answers from heaven, agreement also invites in the **presence** and **power** of God. In fact it literally ushers it in, *For where two or three have gathered together in My name, I am there in their midst (Matt. 18:20)*. Jesus promises to gather to those believers who stand in agreement - it ushers in the presence of God.

Remember the word agree from Amos 3:3 that we looked at earlier? The same word is used at the dedication of Solomon's temple.

And king Solomon, and all the congregation of Israel, who were assembled unto him, were with him before the ark, sacrificing so many sheep and oxen…It happened that when the priests came from the holy place, the cloud filled the house of the Lord, so that the priests could not stand to minister because of the cloud, for the glory of the Lord had filled the house of the Lord (1 Kings 8:5, 10, 11).

Scripture tells us that the people "assembled unto" Solomon. This phrase "assembled unto" is the same word used for agree. The people literally came together in agreement and unity with Solomon. In that atmosphere of agreement the glory of the Lord came down so powerfully that the priests could not stand to minister. If we want to see the glory of God released in our day, we must learn and value the power of agreement!

AGREE WITH THE RIGHT PEOPLE

It is important to have the right relationships. One positive, committed relationship is much more powerful than dozens of acquaintances. The power of agreement is not about how many people are supporting us, but about being in relationship with the right people. The bible says that when we walk in agreement, our effectiveness is multiplied.

I remember the first time I experienced the power of agreement and the corporate anointing that came with it. We were part of an apostolic team in England and the team asked me to go to Liberia to check out a ministry that wanted to connect with us. As I began the meetings that had been arranged for me, I realized that I was operating at a higher level of spiritual release. Almost all the sick that I prayed for were being healed and I found myself looking at my hands a few times because of the anointing that was being released.

One of the most dramatic healings happened late one night. I was staying in a village miles from any civilization and a couple of nights after I had arrived, the chief of the village asked me to come to his home and pray for his wife who was gravely ill. I went with the interpreter and prayed over her and as far as I could tell nothing happened. However, when I woke up the next morning there was a stir in the village. We found out that during the night Jesus came and sat on the foot of the woman's bed and told her that it was He who was healing her, not the white man. Instantly, she was healed and the whole village was opened to the gospel.

I had traveled many times before, but this was the first time I had been sent out as part of a team and the increase in anointing was obvious. When we walk in agreement with others, there is a **corporate anointing** that we step into which greatly increases our effectiveness. If the world is to be reached, it is going to require us coming into relationships with others who carry diverse anointings, because together we will achieve more than we ever would have alone.

POSITIVE OR NEGATIVE AGREEMENTS

Agreement is a powerful thing either in the positive or in the negative. In the positive it ushers in the presence and purpose of God and causes us to walk in fellowship with others. Unfortunately, because it is a law of God, it also works in the negative to produce things that are not of God and can end up separating us from God and eventually from one another. People for centuries have joined organizations, unions, political movements and even gangs all because there is power in agreement. Even when the focus of these organizations is ungodly, there is still power in agreement.

The story of the tower of Babal is one of the most powerful examples in Scripture of negative agreement. As we read the story we see that their motive was to make a name for themselves and the unifying factor God saw was one language and one purpose. When God looked at the negative agreement, He acted to disrupt their unity. *But the Lord came down to see the city and the tower that the men were building. The Lord said, "If as one people speaking the same language they have begun to do this, then nothing they plan to do will be impossible for them* (Gen. 11:5, 6 NIV).

The issue of Babal is that they had come into agreement, but it was an agreement around the wrong things. God's answer was to confuse the language so that the communication necessary to walk in agreement would be hindered. Let us look at verse 6 again, *nothing they plan to do will be impossible for them.* Wow, coming into **agreement has the power to make the impossible possible.**

If this is true in the negative, how much more true is it for those of us who find unity in the Spirit? If from a motive of selfishness and making a name for themselves, people can find a unity that makes the impossible possible, then how much more can those who have been made one in Him find a unity that transcends division and ushers in a culture where the impossible finally becomes normal? **The unifying factor should be to make a name for King Jesus; the one language should be to speak what heaven is speaking, and the one purpose should be to see His glory fill the earth.**

As believers we must remember that agreement is powerful, whether positive or negative. Paul tells the Roman Christians that they would become slaves to the ones they obey. *Do you not know that when you present yourselves to someone as slaves for obedience, you are slaves of the one whom you obey, either of sin resulting in death, or of obedience resulting in righteousness?* (Rom. 6:16) The agreements we make affect more than just our lives but also the lives of everyone around us. In the negative it separates us from God and eventually from others. In the positive it ushers in the presence and purpose of God and causes us to walk in fellowship with others.

All agreements need to start with the agreement we have come into with Christ as a result of the blood. John 15:7 says that if we abide in him (Jesus) and His word abides in us, then we can ask what we will and He promises that it will be done by God the Father. The agreements we have with Him come backed with all the resources of heaven...all of heaven is at the disposal of God on behalf of the individual.

AGREEMENT: JUST ADD GRACE

The power of agreement is only as good as the person's word. A contract, handshake or word of mouth agreement is only as good as the character of the person the agreement is made with. Even in church life all of us have experienced moments when those closest to us found it expedient to change the agreements they had made. The broken promises that accompany this irresponsible behavior have damaged the Body of Christ and have hindered the progress of the Gospel, keeping it from penetrating society as it was intended.

JUST ADD GRACE

The writer of Hebrews makes the importance of grace in relationship clear when he wrote, *"See to it that no one comes short of the grace of God; that no root of bitterness springing up causes trouble, and by it many be defiled"* (Heb. 12:15). If we lose grace for one another, agreement becomes almost impossible and the resulting broken relationships bring great defilement to the body of Christ.

The Webster dictionary states that our English word *agree* comes from a combination of two Latin root words *ad* meaning "to" and *gre* meaning "good will or **grace**." Thus, agreement is found when grace is added into the situation or into the relationship. This is an important concept for any who want to walk in true agreement. I have never known a relationship where it was not necessary to run to grace occasionally in order to maintain agreement. Grace allows us to grow together and develop deep friendships, because implicit in the agreement is the grace to fail. **When we give each other grace, even when we say the wrong thing or act selfishly, the grace is there to cover our weakness and keep the relationship alive and healthy.**

INCOMPLETE BY DESIGN

CHAPTER 9
PARTNERS
FOUNDATIONS FOR TEAM

We work together as partners who belong to God
1 CORINTHIANS 3:9 NLT

Sally and I were both in college, preparing to go to the mission field, when a friend asked if we would fill the pulpit for a church that had lost their pastor. We agreed and for a few weeks drove out and did their Sunday service. Sally played the piano and led the singing and I preached. After several weeks I guess we met their approval and they asked us if we would serve as their pastor. We agreed and they called us. It was the beginning of an interesting learning experience!

The church was basically comprised of two families who always sat on their own side of the building and we had noticed that they seldom spoke to one another. But, we did not know about the feud until after we accepted the position. Both families had put a substantial amount of money into the church building, then at some point they had fallen out and refused to reconcile. By the time we got there it had been going on for years and both sides were entrenched, standing their ground in the hope that the other family would leave first.

It all came out as we tried to pastor our little congregation. If we went to Sunday lunch with one of the families, the next service the other family would hardly speak to us. Then, when we began to visit the community and invite new people into the church, a few came, but none of them would stay. We soon realized that when new ones came into the building, depending on which side of the room they sat, the other family would run them off. They did not want the other side of the church to grow. It would have been funny if it wasn't so sad, and we were relieved when God moved us on.

Our time in this divided house birthed in us a desperate hunger for real unity in the work of God. It would be several years before we understood the value of working together as teams, but Sally and I began our ministry life together by learning to work as partners in an intensely difficult situation.

PARTNERSHIP

In the chapter on fellowship we saw how the biblical concept of fellowship includes the idea of partnership. Now, let's apply that truth into our understanding of team ministry. Paul described our relationship as leaders in the body of Christ as a partnership. He told the church at Corinth that; *We work together as partners who belong to God* (1 Cor. 3:9 NLT). The partnership we walk in has both a vertical and horizontal component. First, I am partnered with Christ in the fulfillment of His commission; He promised His disciples - and by extension to us - that He would be with them and us in partnership till the end of the age (Matt. 28:18). Secondly, we are called to work in partnership with our brothers and sisters who choose to walk in obedience to this commission. This means that we cooperate with one another to fulfill the mutual goal of making Jesus King and filling the earth with His glory!

In the current advancement of the Kingdom of God, it will prove essential that we embrace a fresh and more comprehensive understanding of this partnership. This understanding should influence our leadership model and provide the tools and grace to bridge all ethnic, gender and social boundaries. The limited understanding that we have walked in up to this time has failed to provide the team dynamic necessary to mobilize the troops and finish the task. In the rest of this chapter we offer four foundational principles for building leadership teams in the local church or in any team ministry context. *Common vision, linking of hearts, placement and unselfish sacrifice* are like the four corner pillars in team leadership structure. You can do without one or maybe two of them for a while as long as no storm blows. But if we want to build a leadership team that can stand the tests of adversity, then all four need to be in place for our teams to feel secure and to accomplish their purpose.

COMMON VISION

This principle answers the question: ***Are we going the same direction?*** We partner when we agree to walk and work together to fulfill a common goal. A great challenge for any leadership team is developing and maintaining a clear focus on their goals or vision. Vision gives the people a direction and goals move them toward their purpose in God. Vision gives people a glimpse of the future and invites them to commit their lives as a part of something great. If done right, it will engage and motivate people to work together. A vision needs to be big enough to inspire and yet detailed enough that it can apply to each department in the church or ministry. Without a clear direction that inspires hope, motivating people to follow will prove difficult if not impossible.

Sally and I were once asked to step in to pastor a church that was literally disintegrating. We wouldn't have chosen to do it, but we had so many confirmations that we knew it was God. I had asked in the interview process if the church had any kind of vision statement and found out that they did not. In my first meeting with the leadership as their pastor, I asked each of them to write down for me their understanding of the vision for the church. I intended to spend some time reading them through to find the common elements as a starting place for getting us all on the same page. However, as I read through their visions, I found absolutely no commonality. One wanted a homeschool church, another wanted to be an Assembly of God church, another wanted us all to just love Jesus, and another felt we should join the word of faith movement. I had known we faced some trouble when we took the position but with this one exercise, the reason for the division in the church became obvious.

I soon discovered that the pastor, a very gifted man, had chosen leaders from the various factions in the church and made them all elders. It worked for a while because he was a strong leader and able to hold the various groups together. But over time the tensions began to grow and, as soon as he left, the people scattered. Without a cohesive vision, the divided leadership team literally tore the church apart.

The prophet Amos wrote, *can two people walk together without agreeing on the direction* (Amos 3:3 NLT). It is impossible to walk together unless we are going the same direction. The Hebrew word *agree* here means "to fix upon" which gives the idea that agreement comes as we work at, or negotiate with each other until we have found common ground. Once we come to agreement, walking together becomes relatively easy because we know the direction. The word *agreement* also has a very strong relational and commitment meaning. It carries the idea of building a lasting relationship, which will produce something.

For the body of Christ, there is an overall vision for the church given by Jesus that provides the starting place for the vision of each local church. We each need to understand our part in God's plan and to know what He has called us to in order to establish our priorities. The frequent mistake we see comes when the local vision is so limited that it leaves no room for people to dream. This causes the creativity in the church to get stifled.

This problem of limited vision causes great difficulties for people trying to find their place in the body. If our vision is too small, it restricts the context for developing a leadership team and limits the opportunities for growth. So, if our vision is for a cell group, then get a vision for the church. If our vision is for the church, then get a vision for the city. If it is for the city, then get it for the nation and if we are limited to the nation, get a vision for the world.

Christ's final instructions to His disciples give the starting point for our vision - "Go make disciples of all nations." If the church wants to develop a team ministry model, then we must understand that team will not function effectively outside of embracing and living for the fulfillment of God's promise. If you want team ministry, get a vision for the nations and you will have created an atmosphere broad enough that team can grow.

The Great Commission - to disciple nations - has the power to keep us together and moving in the same direction. Pursuing God's vision calls for more than planting a local church; it urges us to transform our cities. It requires more than evangelism; it compels us to learn how to shape our culture and see the kingdom of God invade every area of society. It involves more than sending out a few missionaries; it engages us in discipling the nations. It goes beyond mission trips; it equips us for the task of developing apostolic teams in every nation. Only this breadth of vision will capture the hearts of this generation and provide the opportunities for each one to get involved.

DIVERSITY OF GIFT

This breadth of vision also makes room for a diversity of gifts. Different gifts see different aspects of the vision. Just as light reflects off different facets of a diamond, each gift views the same situation from a different perspective. So we must come to understand and celebrate the different perspectives, while holding to a common vision. Many teams fail because they do not recognize the value of these different perspectives, and they try to get the whole team to see the leader's point of view. This kind of team will end up being a bland mixture of giftings held together by a strong leader's perspective, rather than common vision.

Inherent in our understanding of fivefold ministry is the concept of diversity in team. No single ministry can adequately express the full image and nature of Christ, any more than a single facet of a diamond can fully reflect the beauty and quality of the whole stone. No single ministry gift has the grace or anointing to function independent from the others, even if it is spectacular. All five ministries are essential to bring the body to maturity. This means that teams built around a single ministry gift will inevitably end up focused on the development of individual ministry, rather than the fulfillment of the vision of Christ.

A key to leading a diverse team comes with understanding the difference between direction and style. Vision has to do with direction and not the style of ministry. Team ministry should not cause a suppression of individual style; rather, it should celebrate the beauty of diversity. The more diversity there is on a team, the greater its effectiveness, and at the same time, the greater its challenges. The easiest team to build and manage is a homogeneous unit. However, this falls far short of the reconciliation on God's heart. Jesus' death on the cross broke down every barrier that would separate His church. Divisions must bow - whether, male or female, Jew or Gentile, black or white, along with any social, economic or religious division.

LINKING OF HEART

This second principle answers the question: **Has God placed us together?** I told the story of our first church at the beginning of this chapter. It has always intrigued us that the two sides came into unity in voting us in, but there was no heart connection between the groups or to us. I think both families thought we appeared too young and naive to prove a real threat and they were probably right. Despite lots of effort, all our work there came to nothing because there was no fellowship between the two families and no desire to reconcile.

To work together in team, members must come to an understanding of the implications of the New Covenant on our relationships in the Kingdom of God. Too often we have treated lightly our commitment to one another, resulting in a fractured and ineffective church. To work as a team there must be a commitment to walk together combined with a willingness to go deeper than just a surface relationship. It must also include a commitment to stay together even when it gets rough. The strength of this commitment comes from knowing that God has put us together because, if we aren't sure He did so, it will prove very difficult to make it work.

Relationships are the key! The body of Christ is not an organization but a living organism. A living organism grows by the development of relationships rather than by a focus on job descriptions or titles. We see this when Paul tells the church that the relational component of unity begins in love. *Beyond all these things put on love, which is the perfect bond of unity* (Col. 3:14). God's unconditional love applied to our relationships will give us a unity that bridges our differences and binds us together.

In the human body, the ligaments hold two parts together to form a joint. Paul applies this same imagery to the body of Christ. *And not holding fast to the head, from whom the entire body, being supplied and held together by the joints and ligaments, grows with a growth which is from God* (Col. 2:19). As we live in close communion with our Lord Jesus, then the rest of our relationships will function in order. Look at that verse again, the entire body gets its life from the head and is held together by the joints and ligaments. These ligaments represent the committed relationships we must develop and maintain if we hope to fulfill our purpose.

What does this look like in practice? There must be some measure of heart commitment that includes several key ingredients. The first is a culture of honor that gives value while allowing openness and honesty. We have all found ourselves in relationships where we walk on eggshells with each other, afraid that we will say or do the wrong thing. For team ministry to work we must get beyond these insecurities and get to a place where honest discussion can happen.

The second component is loyalty and trust. One of our greatest fears in life is disloyalty, and anyone who has been in leadership in the church has had ample opportunity to experience the pain of betrayal first hand. The fear this produces can cause us to avoid deep relationships. For team ministry to function in the local church or on a more regional level, we must find the grace to walk in forgiveness and accept that others will disappoint us in the same way that we disappoint them.

To fulfill our mission we must decide to work with one another determined to always look for the best in each other. Deliberately choosing to see Christ in others by consciously focusing on their strengths and not their weaknesses. God has made provision for this! He set the value of a person when He paid for them with the price of His Son. That means we do not focus on the failures but on the Christ that lives in each of us. Jesus' instruction requires that we, *treat others the same way you want them to treat you* (Luke 6:31). This puts a demand on our relationships. Walking in real covenant relationships means treating people with respect and honor, deliberately giving to them the affirmation we ourselves would like to receive. This kind of honor breathes life into our relationships and links our hearts together.

PLACEMENT

The third principle answers the question: **Where do I fit?** It is essential that each member of the body of Christ finds his or her place, discover their gifts, and come to terms with their strengths and weaknesses. Gathering people is easy; helping them find a place for their gift to fit and function takes a lot of work. We have met many leaders who struggle to raise up the next generation of leaders. The problem is usually not a lack of the right people but a failure to put the right people in the right jobs. Many leave the church and look elsewhere because we have failed to help them develop their gift and find their place.

Paul spoke to this issue of placement when he wrote the Ephesians. *From whom the whole body, being fitted and held together by that which every joint supplies, according to the proper working of each individual part, causes the growth of the body for the building up of itself in love* (Eph. 4:16). As members and leaders in the Body of Christ we are both fitted and held together. We will function at our best in the right position. When I fit securely next to you, the Christ in you completes the gifts and perspective that I lack. At the same time the deposit of Christ in me completes the gifts and perspective that is lacking in you. When we find out where we fit, we discover an effectiveness of purpose that we will never find individually.

Paul goes on to say that not only are we fitted together but that we are **held** together by the supply that flows through the joint. When we get into correct alignment, there is a supply of the life of God that flows into and through us, from and to each other. The strength of team ministry comes from this supply of the life of God that flows through us so that together we achieve more and produce more than we could ever do alone.

Through the joints in the body we receive a supply of all we need to fulfill our purpose and destiny in God. In the body we cannot function as independent vessels seeking to fulfill a divine purpose. We were created interdependent by God's design; we need one another so that we can receive from and give to those around us the supply that is needed. This makes placement in the body absolutely critical. If we never find our place, then we will miss some of the supply that is needed and others will miss the supply they would have received from us had we been in the right position.

Supply flowing to and from each part as God intends, requires a revelation of the value and indispensable nature of each person. This value system provides the foundation for what we call a culture of honor. Paul describes this culture to the Romans. *Be devoted to one another in brotherly love; give preference to one another in honor* (Rom. 12:10). Honor flowing from love causes us to value one another in such a powerful way that we naturally begin to prefer one another. This gives birth to the realization that each part is necessary for the whole to function.

A culture of honor sees value in the individual; first, based on the fact that each person has been created in the image of God. This intrinsic value was further affirmed when the Father sent Jesus to redeem humanity with His blood.

His sacrifice set the worth of each individual as priceless. Next, a culture of honor recognizes the fact that God trusted each member of the body and valued them so highly that He put His Spirit in them! This makes it possible for us to see Christ in each person rather than focusing on their brokenness. Finally, a culture of honor looks at the gifts that have been given to the individual and finds a place for them to function.

With this value system in place, it makes working together and preferring one another flow naturally. The word *prefer* from our key verse has a number of roots. It can mean to lead the way or to take the lead in showing honor. It also conveys the idea of putting another person forward, advancing them and promoting them. Then from the Latin root we get the idea of carrying them in front of us. In an atmosphere of preferring one another the question is never, "Is it my turn?" but rather, "Who is best at this?" As important as placement is, it must never become a self-focused pursuit.

We should expect this kind of preferring one another to flow in the body of Christ between individuals in a local body. It should also flow between departments in the local church. It should flow between churches in a city. It should flow between different teams and streams of ministry. Honor provides an indispensable atmosphere for bringing the body into a functional unity and it begins with knowing where each person fits. This means that the supply we need is in some way dependent on the unity of the body.

The unity needed for us to find each other is not achieved by human reason, nor can it be found in any form of lowest common denominator compromise. Unity is first and foremost a byproduct of the presence of God. Jesus said, *I have given them the glory that you gave me, that they may be one as we are one* (John 17:22 NIV). The presence of His Glory is the key to unity. When the glory of God is present among us, there is an atmosphere of oneness released that makes it easy for us to fit together. So, although we each need desperately to find our place in the body, it is not about us individually; it is about His presence.

UNSELFISH SACRIFICE

The final principle we will look at in this chapter answers the question: ***Are team members willing to pay the price?*** It is easy to offer a person a position of leadership; it is more difficult to get them to be willing for it to cost them something. Most people come into relationships with a mindset of what is it going to do for them? How is it going to benefit their church or their ministry? The truth is that in the kingdom the primary focus is not on ourselves but on the good of the other person.

To function as a team there must be a willingness to sacrifice our own desires for the good of the team. There should be a heart commitment that places Christ and His people above team members' own desires, ambitions and opinions. This paradigm is a by-product of our understanding of servant leadership. The heart of Christ was to serve, not to be served. He describes His disposition when He said; *…the Son of Man did not come to be served, but to serve, and to give His life a ransom for many* (Matt. 20:28). Jesus gave His life for others, thus setting a standard for the activity and actions of leadership in His body.

The obvious tension here is between seeing ourselves as royal sons and daughters of the king while at the same time living our lives before others as servants who are willing to pay the price for their freedom.

IT IS NOT ABOUT YOU

The purpose of team is not to serve as a support group for my encouragement. Team is not for the development of my ministry. In fact it is not about me; it is about Him. Now, as a byproduct of serving together in team, personal development will take place, but the primary goal must be to fulfill His purpose. At the same time team dramatically increases effectiveness as each member of the team uses their strengths and lets their weaknesses be covered. Effective teams draw on the gift and life of God in each member and make a conscious decision to cover one another's weaknesses. In a team that has learned this kind of sacrifice, it is not about taking turns; it is about His purpose being fulfilled. It is not about a position; it is about giving ourselves for others.

Team ministry requires that we take up our cross daily. To walk as Jesus walked involves a cost. It is easier to work individually, but the effective way is to work together with my brothers and sisters. Teamwork has been the source of our greatest joy and some of our deepest pain. It is worth the cost if we know where we belong and have a conviction that God has placed us together for His purpose and for our good. With this confidence and a commitment to stay through the rough times, team becomes exponentially effective.

CHAPTER 10
TEAMWORK
UNITY TO UNIT

That they may be one, just as We are one
JOHN 17:22

Jesus prayed that unity in His body would come to perfection. *I in them and You in Me, that they may be perfected in unity* (John 17:23). The glory of this promise demonstrates that Christ in us is the key to unity. The apostle Paul defines his labor, and by implication, ours in these same terms, *My children, with whom I am again in labor until Christ is formed in you* (Gal. 4:19). He desired that the life of Christ would grow in us individually and corporately until it produced Godhead-like unity in the body. This organic unity is not uniformity. It comes as a byproduct of Christ's life lived out in and through us despite our diversity. Barriers such as rich or poor, male or female, young or old, black or white, Jew or Arab are transcended in Him, as He brings us to the one new man. We find a pictorial illustration of this transition in the book of Judges.

A LOAF OF BARLEY BREAD

Remember the story of Gideon and his magnificent victory over the Midianites. After God did some corporate downsizing, he found his army of 32,000 reduced to 300. God weeded out the fearful and the inattentive, leaving only those He selected for the mission. Even though Gideon had clear direction from the Lord, he still felt nervous. They faced a big army!

On the night before the attack the Lord told Gideon that if he wanted, he could take his servant and go down to the camp. When they got close enough, they could hear a couple of the Midianites discussing a dream one of them had the night before. In the dream a loaf of barley bread rolled down the hill and demolished their camp. Immediately, his friend interpreted the dream as the sword of Gideon and sure enough the next day they were routed.

Think for a moment about the symbolism God uses to illustrate the process He took Gideon through to build his team. A loaf of bread - individual grains of wheat ground into flour then mixed together with other ingredients and thrown into the fire. What a painful process for a grain of wheat, but necessary steps to becoming a loaf of barley bread. God's analogy is full of beautiful symbolism for the process of building a team. The team God wants to build in the local church will have this kind of oneness. It may prove challenging to get there, but the aroma of fresh baked bread when the process is complete makes it all worth it!

The quality of this oneness is clearly defined by Jesus: *The glory which You have given Me I have given to them, that they may be one, just as We are one* (John 17:22). Here, Christ prayed for a unity among us of the same glorious nature as the oneness He experiences in the Trinity - three different Persons with different roles, functions and even identities and yet completely One.

The Greek word *hen* translated "unity" in John 17:23 can also be translated as "one, union or unit." With the word *unit* substituted into the original verse, it reads, "perfected into a unit." When I first saw this, the idea of our unity being transformed into a unit captured my imagination. How wonderful that in creation God created us as a single unit, then separated us out into parts (male and female) and now asks us to come back together and function as one!

TEAMWORK UNITY TO UNIT

The normal usage of the word unit describes an emergency response unit or even a military unit. The implication is of a tightly knit and highly trained group of individuals who take on the most difficult tasks. The concept of a unit highlights many of the characteristics of the perfected unity that God asks us to step into. Here are just a few to get us started.

CHARACTERISTICS OF A UNIT

- A unit has a very clearly defined purpose and is focused on a single task. Priorities are set based on the unit's objective.
- A unit understands team. Many individuals functioning as one, they each know their place, their job, and are ready to use their gift for the good of the whole.
- A unit trains together so that they will understand one another's strengths and weaknesses while learning to work together.
- A unit has a high degree of cross-training where members of the unit train in each area so that, if one drops out, the unit can still function.
- A unit functions with one mind, because they understand lines of authority and can be moved as a group with a single command.
- A unit can respond immediately, because they are prepared for any circumstance no matter how difficult. They are on constant watch.
- A unit has no room for pretense; in a unit you either know how to do the job or you do not. You cannot fake being a brain surgeon or helicopter pilot.
- A unit understands the need for good communication and develops mechanisms to ensure that each member gets the information that they need.
- A unit develops a high level of trust. They focus on their own task and do not waste time second-guessing or micro-managing others on the team.
- A unit has learned to turn competition into cooperation so that the healthy drive to excel is turned for the good of the whole.

The task for us as leaders is to apply these same principles to our life and ministry in the body of Christ. The Word challenges us to move from talking about unity to actually becoming a unit. This proves critically important, because we have an emergency. The world does not know Jesus and our single purpose is to make Jesus King. Millions die each year without the benefit of the message we carry, and on some level they wait for the body to get itself together and begin to function in team and as a unit.

Now we can better understand why Paul warns the church to be *diligent to preserve the unity of the Spirit in the bond of peace* (Eph. 4:3). Deliberately protecting the unity of the Spirit is essential for us to see the harvest of souls on the scale we believe for.

CHARACTERISTICS OF EFFECTIVE TEAM

Now let's look at some practical steps we can take in developing team ministry with a goal of transforming our leadership into a functioning unit. Teams do not form automatically. In fact, in many ways teamwork goes against our nature, especially with the individualism of our culture. So, care and understanding will prove necessary for effective team building that fulfills its purpose. From our experience of leading and being a part of several leadership teams, we have identified the following characteristics that influence the effectiveness of team ministry.

SECURE LEADERSHIP

The establishment and building of a leadership team depends on secure leadership. This means that the leader of a team must be selected carefully and should have an evident touch from God in order to be able to carry the hearts of the other team members. Because insecurity always exalts self, the leader needs to be substantially free from insecurities so he or she can make room for other gifts. An insecure leader will delegate very little to others. This leads to frustration in the other team members, restricting them so that the team never gets the value of their input or gifts.

The team leader must also have an understanding of the difference between delegated authority and earned respect. All authority in the church belongs to Jesus and He anoints some with the mantle of leadership, delegating to them a measure of spiritual authority. However, even though we may have been given the authority to lead by Christ, **we must still earn the respect of those we lead by our behavior**. No matter how much authority we carry, we still must treat those that follow us with respect and honor. If, as John Maxwell says, leadership really is influence, then it is up to us to live our lives in such a way that others will want to be influenced by us.

Finally, each team member must have an understanding of spiritual authority. When each of us yields to God's delegated authority with open hearts, leading a team becomes a joy. This willingness to submit to one another is the bedrock of serving together. The pride that keeps us from yielding to authority always divides, while humility unites. This means that humility will always serve as an anchor point for our walk from unity to unit.

PRESENCE DRIVEN

A team leader has the authority to make a final decision in times when a team gets deadlocked. But, if this becomes the normal pattern for decision-making in team life, something is wrong. The goal for any leadership team should be to make presence-driven decisions. By this we mean that the team would have confidence that they have heard one another and of more importance they have heard the voice of the Holy Spirit before reaching a decision. This is not the same as consensus.

The popular move to a consensus form of leadership has some value, but it tends to produce a lowest common denominator kind of unity and lacks the clarity necessary to move a church or ministry forward. On the other hand, Spirit-motivated decision making gives the opportunity for all the members of the team to hear heaven and respond with a solution that originates with the Spirit. The challenge for any team is that the busyness of making decisions can quickly rob the team of the time needed in the presence of God and will result in intellectually driven decisions.

To achieve presence driven decisions, the leader needs to understand the difference between an authoritarian and a consultative leadership style. An authoritarian leader uses the team, but lacks the grace needed to unlock the potential in the other team members. A more consultative leadership style lets the members of the team have input. The goal is not simply to come to decisions but to decide based on what heaven is saying. What confidence we would have if we did not make a decision until we all knew we had heard God!

RECIPROCAL HELP

The willingness to offer mutual help is another crucial characteristic of an effective team. As a team works together with a genuine desire to release the gifts in each member, it builds a common desire for each individual to succeed. As this happens, members of the team will eagerly work together to accomplish the goals set for them. They believe that together they can accomplish the impossible. In this positive atmosphere, should someone struggle or fail at their task, the power of team means that mistakes are covered and the goal gets accomplished through the group's willingness to work as a whole.

We need to understand that in so doing some measure of individuality will get sacrificed for the good of working together as a whole. This atmosphere helps us begin to understand the Scripture: *Rejoice with those who rejoice, and weep with those who weep* (Rom. 12:15). This team mindset leads us to believe that if he or she wins, then we win because of our connection to one another. When we begin to see ourselves in this kind of interdependent relationship, we can expect the synergy to produce a dramatic increase in effectiveness.

Synergy can be defined as "the whole is greater than the sum of the parts." In other words, with synergy it is possible for a team to do more together than the sum total of their individual strengths and abilities. One of the more popular acronyms for team is "Together Everyone Achieves More." This proves true for those who will truly give themselves to the process of learning to work effectively with others. When the team functions correctly, they do achieve more through the synergy that multiplies the output, as together they carry the load.

CORPORATE IDENTITY

Members in an effective team will have made the shift from focus on their individual or ministry advancement to a corporate way of thinking. This identity shift means that members of the team find their satisfaction in fulfilling the goals of the team. There will also be a high degree of loyalty toward other team members and team decisions. One my favorite acronyms for team is *Taming Ego Activates Mission*. If we can tame our ego and learn to think as part of the team, we will see a dramatic increase in the effectiveness of our leadership team and move toward becoming a unit.

One of the most noticeable effects of this shift is in the way team members communicate team decisions. They use the pronoun "we" instead of "they" or "I". This change in vocabulary protects the integrity of the team's unity and purpose. One of the most destructive things we can do to a team is to walk out from a meeting and say "they" decided! When we do this, we separate ourselves out of the team in an attempt to distance ourselves from the decision and win favor. Undermining behavior such as this is profoundly disloyal. Even if we do not totally agree with the decision, as part of the team we have a responsibility to honor the corporate decision.

We can see this demonstrated in Acts, where a deep division threatened the early church. At issue was how much of the Jewish Law the Gentile believers were going to be required to keep. After all the discussion, James stood up and gave a summary of the decision: *For it has seemed good to the Holy Spirit and to us…* (Acts 15:28). Once they reached a decision, all the team carried out that decision even though opinions ran strong.

OPEN DISCUSSION

A team cannot operate at its full potential without open discussion. The communication within the team should take place in a safe and supportive atmosphere that encourages interaction in the process of decision-making or problem-solving. If we want good information when we make decisions, we must create a safe environment where people can brainstorm without disparagement.

When we have this kind of open environment, it stimulates creativity and accelerates the growth of the team. We will always reach better decisions if we have access to all the wisdom and creativity in the group. When we allow everyone to input, we communicate his or her value to the team. And as long as they feel heard, they will thrive, because they know that their ideas have at least been given consideration.

The context of leadership meetings must remain secure enough that sensitive issues can be shared and discussed openly. This requires the team leader to create an environment where each member understands the need for confidentiality. Team members must be able to open up with one another without fear of reprisal and with the confidence that the discussion will stay in the room. We must also feel secure in the knowledge that things we share will not be used against us at a later date.

CULTURE OF HONOR

A culture of honor in the church or leadership team is based on the application of heaven's value system to our relationships and responses. The value system present in many church cultures measures the usefulness of a person based on what they do for us. There is a legitimate honor based on giving our lives in service to Jesus, but, if this is the only basis for honor in the church, it degenerates to works-based affirmation.

The word *honor* in the New Testament means value or more specifically the value based on price paid. Now it gets interesting! The value of an object is not based on what we think it is worth, but on what someone is willing to pay for it. God set the value of a human being when He paid the price of the blood of His Son for every individual. So, the honor they are due has little or nothing to do with how valuable they appear to us or even how much they do for us. Their value was set by the purchase price and that makes them priceless. If people really are priceless, then we need to treat them with value and deference no matter who they are or what they have done.

Paul told the Roman believers that they were to: *give preference to one another in honor* (Rom. 12:10). The word *preference* here means, "to take the lead." So Paul's injunction is that we must "take the lead in showing honor." It is the responsibility of every leader to find ways to show honor to the other members of the team. This can be done in a variety of ways, starting with the way we speak, the way we respond and especially the way we react when things do not quite go our way.

When we apply this to our interactions as a leadership team, each member of the team should feel received as a valued part of the team. During the discussion in our meetings, each member should feel that they have been heard and leave the meeting knowing that their opinion had merit and had been given honest consideration even if not fully implemented. The way we treat one another in this context is a clear reflection of the way we as leaders will treat the body. So use the leadership team as the proving ground for honor so that it becomes the culture of the whole church body.

CROSS TRAINING

In a military unit cross training is a fundamental part of becoming a unit. Each member of the team goes through the process of learning the specialty skills of every other member so that if someone is out of commission for any reason, the objective of the team can still be completed. We need to bring elements of this same process into our church leadership teams.

There should also be a high degree of cross training within a leadership team so that each member understands the function and role of the other members. They also need to understand the process for decision-making. When a team member is unavailable for any reason, others can step up and carry the load as long as necessary. This process of cross training ensures that we achieve the goals of the team even when an individual member experiences sickness or difficulty.

For this to work, we must each be secure enough to allow others into our realm without fear that they will undermine our position. Too often insecurity in individual members of a team blocks this process - insecurities motivated by fear.

REGULAR COMMUNICATION

In a team leadership context, the members of the team function in different areas of ministry. These diverse responsibilities make the flow of information between the members essential. For the team to function well and stay together they must focus on communication. Lack of information is the most common cause of unrest in a team. The leader must put mechanisms in place so that all the members of the team get regular updates from the different departments; then they will all feel involved even if members miss a meeting. Keeping them up to date on decisions that were made communicates value and keeps the whole team engaged in the process.

Because information has great value and ensures that the team stays together, each member of the team should be encouraged to communicate fully and frankly. They need to understand that decisions the team makes are affected by the quality of the information available. Members who understand this are then eager to hear what others have to say, as well as to give their input.

Information is power and, if members of the team withhold information as a means to maintain control in their area of ministry, then the whole team will be ineffective. The team needs to work together to ensure the proper flow of information so that everyone feels involved and valued.

DEFINED EXPECTATIONS

Unmet or undefined expectations work against the unity of the team and rob our leaders of their motivation. When expectations of the team members toward one another are not clearly laid out, we set people up for disappointment. Much of the dissension in a leadership team can be avoided by defining the expectations we have for one another; this is especially true for the team leader. If as a leader, we fail to spell out the expectations we have of the other leaders, we disable them. Hidden expectations will cause us to doubt others and will cause them to doubt our commitment to help them succeed.

Expectations need to be particularly clear when it comes to delegation. We look in depth at this in the next chapter but for now we need to understand that clearly spelled out expectations in advance will communicate value to the team members. While on the other hand, expectations or deadlines communicated during the task or after something has gone wrong will always have the effect of devaluing or demotivating the members of our team.

In a properly functioning team, the individual members will feel secure in making decisions that affect their area, because the boundaries have been well established and the goals and philosophy of the team are clearly understood by each member. The more clearly we define our expectations, the more effectively the team will function.

GENUINE RELATIONSHIPS

The depth of relationships within the team makes the difference between the team functioning as a well-oiled machine or becoming a living organism. As we have seen in a previous chapter, leadership in the church functions as an extension of the government of God, and as the *ecclesia*, it does have an organizational leadership responsibility. However, without *koinonia* (the fellowship component) it will lack life and vitality. For a team to function effectively the members of the team must deliberately build relationships with one another outside of meetings.

There is a saying that familiarity breeds contempt; this has often been the excuse to limit the depth of relationships we pursue as leaders. However, there is no substitute for fellowship time. The longer a leadership team is in existence, the more established relationships become and this familiarity helps develop a relaxed working environment. In such cases the members and leader will have a high degree of confidence and trust in one another and will be willing to yield to one another.

It is also essential that not all the relationship building be focused on the key leader, but with one another. Many groups fail because the relationships between the members of the group will not sustain the level of openness necessary to function as a team. The answer to this is a network of friendships and relationships that connect everyone in the team to the others. The depth of these will inevitably vary, but it ensures that everyone on the team feels connected.

CHAPTER 11
DELEGATION
SHARED RESPONSIBILITY

Entrust these to faithful men who will be able to teach others also
2 TIMOTHY 2:2

Sally and I pastored a church in Ripon, North Yorkshire for several years. The church grew rapidly and a large leadership team came together. Things went well for the first couple of years, but over time we began to experience some struggles in the leadership. At first they had all seemed eager to help and carry responsibility, but gradually this changed. Things that I assigned them wouldn't get done, and I frequently had to step in and fix things or finish something that had been half done. Eventually, we got to the point that I felt ready to ditch all of them and start over.

Several members of the church we pastored worked as trainers at a facility near us, which did weekend retreats with corporate leaders.[8] These leaders were taken through exercises to help them develop in their leadership skills, with a particular emphasis on how to function as teams. One day in frustration I asked Phil, one of the trainers, if he would spend some time with our team and help me understand what had gone wrong.

Phil and I sat down and I explained the problem from my perspective and then left him to do his job. He spent a couple of weeks sitting in our leaders' meetings, as well as, meeting individually with each leader. In hindsight he was a great listener! When he had finished, he called and made an appointment to meet with me again. I was excited because I knew he was going to give me the key to fixing the problem.

But, his opening statement caught me off guard. "Steve, you have created the breakdown in your leadership team!" I felt the wind knocked out of me. Then he went on to explain that the way I delegated caused frustration, restriction and ended up disabling my leaders. I felt a little like David when Nathan the prophet confronted him by telling him a story. Nathan got his attention when he told him that "he was that man." I almost got offended, but I felt the Spirit check me; as much as I did not like the answer, I knew he was right.

Phil helped me see my weakness and then worked with me periodically over the next several months. Miraculously, most of the issues that had been there in the leadership team simply disappeared as I repented and began to learn the art of delegation. Over the years I have come to believe that delegation remains one of the great weaknesses in leadership teams. Much of what we share in this chapter, I learned from Phil. Although to the best of my knowledge I have not quoted him, much of the information in this chapter came from him.

ART OF DELEGATION

Delegation is an art. As with most art, 25% comes from raw talent and 75% from learned ability. This comes as good news for those of us who are not naturally good at delegation. Delegation is an essential leadership skill because it serves as a primary mechanism for moving a church from a one-man leadership model into true team ministry. And as a bonus, delegation done correctly not only builds team, it strengthens the bond of relationship and allows for the development of the potential in every leader.

DELEGATION SHARED RESPONSIBILITY

As we study the art of delegation we want to understand the dynamics for both parties: the delegator, the leader giving the responsibility and the delegatee, the one taking the responsibility. Both must learn to *move beyond simple assignment of tasks, to true delegation.* Much of what we generally think of as delegation has really been little more than handing out jobs to people. **True delegation involves a transfer of ownership**. Delegation requires subtle shifts in thinking and negotiated boundaries, which empower people by giving them the authority to respond to situations without always having to refer back to us. Many leaders want others to take responsibility for areas of ministry but prove reluctant to relinquish control.

Assignment is simply the transfer of something to another that needs to be accomplished. Delegation may well include assignment, but it is an assignment that carries with it the authority to act on behalf of the one delegating. When we delegate something to a person, we have designated them to act for us and to represent us. So when we delegate, we must ensure that they know what we want; we must know that they have the ability to do the job and we must give them the authority they need to complete the assignment.

The original meaning of the word *delegate* was "to send someone authorized to operate on your behalf." So, authorization or authority must change hands for a leader to truly delegate. This is where delegation often breaks down. If we attempt to delegate a job without giving the authority necessary to accomplish the task, we cannot expect the other person to take responsibility. In fact, without the authority to do the job, all we create is frustration.

MIND SHIFTS FOR THE DELEGATOR

This authority/responsibility shift provides the basis for delegation. Both parties must commit to the process of change this requires to avoid frustration and failure. For the delegator, we see four shifts in thinking that will make the transition of responsibility work naturally.

The first change involves the value system we use. Assuming that the delegatee has the necessary skills for the job, we must determine to value more than a person's ability; we must value their insight. If we will trust the intuition of the ones we are asking to take responsibility, it becomes much easier for them to take real ownership.

The second area of change for the delegator moves them from a possessive view of their realm of responsibility to a willingness for joint ownership. A possessive leader will find it difficult to delegate because they hold too tightly to the roles of leadership. Without the offer of joint ownership, it is unrealistic to expect our leaders to take true responsibility for a task. We know many leaders who get frustrated with their team because apparently their team will not take ownership. But when we investigate, we quickly find that the possessive senior leader cannot or will not let go, leaving his or her team in frustration.

The third area of adjustment a leader must make if they want to delegate is to move from insecurity to shared authority. Insecurity has always been one of the biggest challenges of leadership. Because insecurity produces self-focus, it is nearly impossible for an insecure person to navigate the process of delegation successfully. So, if you struggle with insecurity, repent of the self-focus it produces and ask God for the grace to see others through His eyes. We will deal with this more in the next chapter.

The fourth change for the delegator will involve a deliberate move to release creative liberty. We have already seen that we need to trust the intuition of our team, but we must go beyond that and engage the creativity of each member of the team as well. There is a significant difference between asking someone to do it our way and allowing them to put themselves into the task. For the leader this means accepting that different isn't wrong. We will discuss later the idea of setting creative boundaries, but for now understand that without some measure of creativity released to the individual, they will have a difficult time putting their heart and soul into the role they have been given.

DELEGATION SHARED RESPONSIBILITY

MIND SHIFTS FOR THE DELEGATEE

We also see at least four changes that the delegatee will need to make if he or she is going to successfully operate in their new role. The first change involves a mental shift from servitude to ownership. A servant mindset does tasks automatically and, even though they may do it well, they take little interest in how their individual task fits into the whole. Ownership takes a broader view, where we invest ourselves into our specific task with an awareness of how it affects the whole. So, if overlap or even conflict with another person's assignment should occur, we will serve as part of the solution rather than part of the problem.

The second change in the delegatee will involve a move from response to taking responsibility. As servants in the house, we respond to instructions in order to fulfill the expectations of a boss. But when we begin to receive delegated authority, we make the shift from simply following instructions to taking actual responsibility for something being birthed. The difference between responding to instructions and taking responsibility is foundational. A leader who responds to instructions is a vital part of the team, but a leader who takes responsibility adds in his skills and abilities in a unique way that helps move the team forward.

A leader cannot delegate *responsibility*; responsibility is something that must be taken. The word responsibility derives from a combination of two Latin words: *respond* which means "to pledge back" and *able* which means "skill or strength." The Romans used this combination of words as a part of the oath of loyalty that all soldiers took. They pledged their strength and ability to the Emperor as they were drafted into the Roman army. In our terms, responsibility then flows from a decision we made to act out a pledge of loyalty with our ability. No one can <u>make</u> you do it; it is a decision. I can ask you to take responsibility; but in the end, you must choose to take it.

The third shift is a move from simple obedience to one in authority to the godly exercise of authority. Authority can get a little heady. Being in a position where we can exert influence over others must be held as a sacred trust. Unfortunately, we have seen gifted individuals begin to turn their influence into an opportunity for self-promotion. In the parable of the servant who was forgiven a debt, his response to those under him caused him to self-destruct (Matt. 18:21-35). *As we step into authority, we must realize that only someone who willingly operates under authority can ever truly exercise godly authority.*

The final paradigm shift for the delegatee is a move from duty to opportunity. Jesus told a parable to his disciples about the shift from servant to son. The heart of the parable showed that the sons would know the will of the father and do it. When we operate out of duty we do the task by rote, following instructions to the best of our ability. A son, however, has the opportunity to build a future based on the trust he has received. Having someone delegate an area of responsibility to us should serve as a great opportunity for our growth and development as a leader. Make the most of it.

THE GRACE TO DELEGATE

God gives us grace for the leadership responsibilities He entrusts to us. Paul speaks of the measure of grace available to us, a measure that expands as the requirements increase. When learning to delegate, we should ask God for an increased measure of grace to allow us to make the changes necessary in our thinking and behavior for delegation to be effective. To develop the grace to delegate, we have identified five broad skill areas that need development. Good delegators will commit to developing in each of these areas. Find the one where you feel weak and start there, but do not stop until they all become normal.

COMMUNICATE CLEARLY THE OBJECTIVE

Good communication makes delegation work. We seldom come across as clearly as we think and, even if we were clear, people hear through different filters and expectations. Communication in this context begins with clearly defining the objectives and at each stage of the defining process asking for feedback. The defining process should involve communicating an answer to some or all of the questions: What? Why? How? When? and Where?

DELEGATION SHARED RESPONSIBILITY

What – lay out the vision: What do you want achieved? Let them inside your head; sell them on the idea; give them a clear picture of what you think it will look like. This is a crucial step because in the process we will recognize things we have overlooked. The open discussion this generates will make the leaders around us feel more secure. If they see and feel that we are approachable, they will more readily offer their input.

Why – help them take ownership: Let them know why this needs to be done. It is almost impossible to take ownership of something that we do not understand. Fit this job into the big picture; explain why this is necessary to accomplish the whole. Servants just follow instructions, but sons need to understand in order to invest themselves into the project. If we want real delegation, we will take the time to lay out the plan in such a way that they can fully buy into it and understand their part and their value to the whole.

How – describe the resources: What resources are you making available to them? Finance, manpower, equipment or workspace, what do they have to work with? If this conversation takes place up front, it limits the surprises and sets realistic expectations. If we restrict the flow of information, resources or even the knowledge they need, it will disable the very people that we want to succeed.

When – layout the timetable: When does this need to be done? If there are stages, define a timetable for each stage. We cause our leaders great frustration when we do not clarify the deadlines we expect. If it needs to be done in a hurry, then make sure they know it and feel willing and able to get it finished on time. By failing to make the timetable clear, we leave our leaders scrambling to complete something that they should have known about much earlier.

Where – venue: Where is this to happen, or Where are they to do this work? What space is available to them? If we do not clarify this, we can easily create issues, especially in a church setting where rooms serve multiple purposes. Some of our greatest conflicts come with the joy of shared space. If we have not made this clear in the beginning, we have no room to blame others for the fallout. The discussion of who will take responsibility to do the negotiating between departments must get clarified.

SET THE CREATIVE BOUNDARIES

Creative boundaries define your expectations and provide the framework for the delegatee to exercise their own ideas. If you want three options to choose from, spell it out in advance so that they know the boundaries of their creative input. Boundaries established in advance communicate safety and trust, while boundaries added as we go communicate failure and tend to de-motivate. Changing the rules midstream is a sure way to create frustration within your leadership team.

God created human beings to create; this means that it is essential in the development of a team that we make room for individual creativity. To set creative boundaries, ask yourself a few questions: How much independent thinking do you want? How much of themselves do you want them to invest? If they come up with a better idea than yours, what process should they follow? In reality, the more minds that look at a problem, the better the solution. So, listen. If they feel you will hear them, they may suggest a better way from the beginning.

This brings up one of the greatest challenges for one who is delegating responsibility. For a leader accustomed to doing things his or her own way, it is essential that we learn that **different isn't wrong** unless clear boundaries have been violated. The leader must make a deliberate decision to accept another person's creative input. In fact, if they find a solution that differs from ours (unless ours has significant benefits), it would be best to reward their effort and give them the benefit of the doubt. This serves as a powerful way to honor them and encourage the best from their creativity.

Often the barrier to this is the leader's own insecurity that insists on things being done "their way". However, this is a dangerously shortsighted approach. If we will deal with our insecurity and open ourselves up to input from the team, we will find a breadth of creative ideas which will make the final outcome much more whole.

DELEGATE THE AUTHORITY

The most common mistake in delegation happens when we ask someone to take on responsibility, but then fail to give them the authority they need to fulfill the task. We would alleviate much of the frustration of leadership if we learned this principle. Remember, as a leader we cannot give a person responsibility, but we can give them authority. The authority resides in the leader, and it is their prerogative to share it with others. **For the leader this shift to genuine shared authority is what makes delegation.** This shift gives ownership and 'right' to the one who has taken the responsibility.

The authority that we delegate should be in proportion to the responsibility that we are asking them to assume. This includes sufficient authority to do the job: the right to spend the resources, the right to recruit the help, and the right to make decisions within creative boundaries. Once this authority has been given, it belongs to them. The delegator must not usurp the authority given to the delegatee. If we see something not getting done and we step in and do it, we have usurped their authority. It does not matter how good our motive, if we do not do this in a way that empowers them, we will destroy their confidence.

If we see them struggling, help them by coming alongside them. Be willing to go with them, show them; whatever we do, it is crucial that we do not just take it from them and do it ourselves. If we will take the trouble and time to help them, they will learn our expectations and know that they have our trust. If we constantly take back what we have given, our leaders will never grow. In fact, it will make them reluctant to accept responsibility in the future because they feel devalued.

ESTABLISH AN ACCOUNTABILITY STRUCTURE

An old saying tells us to "inspect what you expect." For accountability to work, we need to set goals that are both measurable and achievable. Abstract goals produce frustration. Establishing an accountability structure requires forethought. You cannot show up at the meeting with nothing in mind and then come up with something. The failure to think through and plan an accountability structure is a common cause of delegation failure.

The accountability structure that we put in place should reflect maturity. If someone has been beside us for years, they need very little detailed structure. But with someone new to responsibility, it will prove important to set stage goals with built-in feedback at each stage. The design of this accountability structure should help them understand the impact of their work on the work of others. Most of us have tunnel vision and it is our responsibility to help them to see the broader picture. The more leadership experience the delegatee has, the more of this stage of management will pass to them.

In this accountability discussion we must be specific both in expectation and timetable. Setting goals in advance works well, but a hindsight accountability structure communicates failure. When we set goals in advance, we communicate confidence and confidence in the expectations always gives less room for error. For example, in delegating a project we might say, "I would like you to have a rough draft for me to look at next Tuesday. Call me on Friday and let me know how it is going." When they do not call Friday (which they may not), call them Saturday morning early. "Hey, I did not hear from you yesterday." You have laid out your expectations clearly and have followed up in a way that keeps them on track.

The final component of the accountability structure comes with establishing their right of access. If we delegate something to others, they have higher than normal access to us. Make sure cell phone numbers have been exchanged. A common perception is that leaders are too busy to be bothered. We must ensure that those who carry responsibility have sufficient access to us, so that they feel empowered to complete the task.

DELEGATION SHARED RESPONSIBILITY

COMMUNICATE VALUE

The value system present in a culture of honor causes each individual to feel safe to express his or her opinion without fear of criticism. In this environment, conflicting ideas can be discussed without insecurities getting in the way. Often leaders bemoan the fact that they do not get honest feedback. Usually this happens because those they work with simply do not feel safe to open up and share honestly.

When a leader seeks to live with honor as a value, people feel safe, even in the midst of conflict. Leaders who walk in honor refuse to listen to complaints about other members of the team when the one with the complaint has not gone to them first. If people know that we have their backs and know that we will stand with them, it makes them feel like a valued member of the team.

For delegation to work we must communicate and communicate often - not just about things that may go wrong, but about them as people. "I need you as a person, not just your hand to do a job." The more valued they feel the better they will function. For this reason, affirmation always exceeds and precedes any correction that we need to bring. Find the things they are doing right and look for ways to honor their progress.

This emphasis on affirmation has nothing to do with coercion. Manipulation of any kind has no place in delegation. If there is no will to do what you are asking of them, then do not give it to them at all. If they are willing to help but not to take responsibility, then give them an assignment and give them time to gain the confidence to take on real responsibility. It is also important to make sure that they have the ability before you ask them to take on the responsibility for a task. If we do not, we set them up for failure; so use good judgment in assigning a task. Start by giving them something you know they can succeed at. That way we can honestly speak to others of our confidence in them.

The beauty of delegation is that it allows the people on our leadership teams to use and develop their gifts to their fullest potential. Because of this the very act of delegating serves as a means of valuing. Paul challenged Timothy to *entrust these to faithful men who will be able to teach others also* (2 Tim. 2:2). The whole nature of leadership distills down to one thing, the impartation of what we have to others so that they in turn can do the same.

CHAPTER 12
AUTHORITY
UNDER HIS RULE

Have confidence in your leaders and submit to their authority
HEBREWS 13:17 NIV

From the moment Jesus began His ministry He spoke and taught with great authority. As the crowds witnessed the miracles, they were awestruck at His authority (Matt. 9:8). Then when Jesus commissioned His disciples, He described the limitless extent of His authority by declaring that, *All authority has been given to Me in heaven and on earth* (Matt. 28:18). As a result of His complete obedience, all authority in the universe is His. Any authority the enemy had stolen from man or any other realm was stripped from him and it ALL belongs to Jesus.

In the next breath Jesus commissioned His followers to go and make disciples in every nation with the promise that His presence would accompany them. *I am with you always, even to the end of the age* (Matt. 28:20). This promise of His abiding presence follows us as we walk in obedience to His will. As long as we remain under His authority and give ourselves to making disciples both at home and in the nations, He is present with us and in us always. What a promise - all authority in the universe has been given to Jesus and He is with us. By implication then, all authority in the universe is available to us, His co-laborers. His commission gave us authority to act on His behalf, authorizing us to represent Him in the task of extending His kingdom rule on the earth.

As His ambassadors we carry out His instructions and bring heaven's rule into this realm. The authority He gave covers every eventuality; we deal with the works of the evil one by operating in Christ's authority. We release His kingdom, using His authority to change atmospheres. We must also exercise His authority as leaders, representing Him in His body.

Jesus, the model leader, did what He did under the authority of heaven. The principle here is that **in order to exercise authority we must be under authority.** Jesus operated in perfect submission to the Father. His perfect submission released in Him a perfect, unshakable peace in every situation. If Christ knew that He must submit to the Father, how much more do we need to deal with our fears and find where God would have us invest our lives?

Jesus carried amazing authority but remained loving, gentle and compassionate with people. His love drew people to Him even when they messed up. His response to the woman caught in adultery takes our breath away. His act of offering the bread to Judas just before the betrayal sets a standard for servant leadership. In fact, the only times Jesus appeared stern were with the religious leaders who kept others from the truth by their legalism and pride.

One day a centurion came to Jesus and asked Him to heal his servant girl. When Jesus offered to go to his house, he declined and made an astounding statement. *Just say the word, and my servant will be healed* (Matt. 8:8). He then explained why he was so confident. *I also am a man under authority, with solders under me; and I say to this one, go and he goes* (Matt. 8:9). The Centurion saw something in Jesus, which he recognized as obedience to a higher authority. He knew Jesus was a man under authority and he knew that just a word was enough. Jesus described the centurion's understanding of authority as *faith*.

AUTHORITY UNDER HIS RULE

LEADERSHIP AUTHORITY

We find it easy to understand how we use our authority to deal with the works of the enemy - by releasing healing, deliverance, and breaking strongholds. But how does spiritual authority work in the church? But what does spiritual authority look like when applied to our relationships in the body of Christ? Specifically, what does spiritual authority look like in our relationships with church leadership? The writer of Hebrews tells us to *have confidence in your leaders and submit to their authority* (Heb. 13:17 NIV). Verses like this have been abused by some and ignored by others, an indication that we need to better understand the real nature of this spiritual authority. So let's take a walk through this minefield together, shall we?

OUR JOURNEY

We experienced our first encounter with a spiritual father while on the mission field. We had served under pastors in our denominational background and listened to men of God like Ian Thomas and Stewart Briscoe who walked in real spiritual authority. But apart from occasional advice, no one took a specific interest in helping us develop as leaders. We had asked for input several times, but it never developed into anything significant. In fact we soon learned that, if we did open up and expose an area of weakness, it would eventually be used against us.

Our mission background held independence as a core value. I think it ranked up there with cleanliness and godliness. So the idea of submission to any kind of authority seemed like a foreign concept. Of course, as leaders in the work, we wielded great authority over the people we worked with, but it lacked any accountability. Consequently, the rugged, individualistic missionaries (tough enough to work in our area of Kenya) did their own thing. Some proved highly effective while others lived like they had taken an extended holiday. We learned early to keep to ourselves and made sure not to "rock the boat." When we did try to speak into a situation where blatant immorality existed, instead of the situation being dealt with as it should have been, we were cautioned by the area superintendent to back off.

When God filled us with His Spirit, He also gave us a hunger for relationships with real accountability. The situation in which we found ourselves felt unhealthy, and we had no opportunity to receive the guidance we knew we needed. About that time, God in His wisdom relocated us to a town near Nairobi, Kenya. A friend needed an engineer to help produce a new design of windmill. This exciting project brought hope that many of the nation's water wells would be converted over to wind power.

The church on the farm where we lived had developed a relationship with an apostolic ministry. It looked like a perfect set up, and after meeting with the apostle, we both agreed, along with the pastor of the church, to work under his oversight. The church had been pastored by the owner of the farm, which made it a little intimidating for the people who had their boss as their pastor. As soon as we arrived, he asked us to assume that role; that made me the pastor of my boss. Even with the interesting leadership dynamic, we almost immediately stepped into the blessing of God. The Holy Spirit fell in the services and we experienced a time of real revival. Our house was packed every time we called a prayer meeting and we saw many miracles. So many were getting saved at one point that, with the hectic work schedule, we did baptisms in the local lake at midnight with hippos looking on.

Despite the great things God did, we began to struggle with the style of leadership we witnessed from our apostolic oversight. We soon realized that the order of the day was control and his authoritarian manner made working with him a difficult and humbling experience. After a few weeks we began to ask God what we had done to deserve this. We did not want to be rebellious, but his dictatorial "spiritual authority" did not fit with our understanding of Scripture or the nature of Jesus.

Finally, one night it came to a crisis. We desperately wanted to learn the lessons that God had for us in this situation but, quite honestly, did not want to pattern our lives after the example we witnessed. That night the Lord spoke to us clearly that He had not brought us there to model our lives after a person, rather, He had brought us there to learn to pray. Instantly, we felt relief. We truly admired the prayer life of our leader and had no trouble giving ourselves to learn this from him. Even better we had a direction for that season of our lives. How easy submission can be when we know we have heard from God. Eighteen months later God graciously moved us on from there; the mission board revoked our work permit because we wouldn't agree to never speak in tongues in public.

All authority belongs to Jesus and He delegates spiritual authority for the building of His body. The authority He gives is not for controlling or manipulating people in the local church. ***Rather, it is for the releasing of the people of God into their destinies.*** The end product of the correct use of spiritual authority should always be a healthy and mature body. To better understand the nature of spiritual authority exercised in the church we want to look into some specific situations and the kind of authority that is appropriate in each.

THREE KINDS OF AUTHORITY

Sally and I have observed three different kinds of authority that operate in the life of a church and in the work of God. The first is task related, an assignment to be completed that requires someone to take charge and get the job done: we will call this Task Authority. The second authority operates in teaching or training situations with the goal of introducing a principle or practice that needs to be learned. We call this Teaching Authority. Finally, there is an authority necessary in situations where a spiritual or moral principal is at issue. We call this Transformative Authority.

These three aspects of authority roughly line up with Webster's three categories of authority. It is fascinating to note how often Daniel Webster drew on his knowledge of the Bible in developing his definitions. First, "the power to give orders or make decisions: the power or right to direct or control someone or something." Second, "the confident quality of someone who knows a lot about something or who is respected or obeyed by other people." And third, "a quality that makes something seem true or real."

AUTHORITY AND OBEDIENCE

The New Testament uses three primary words for obedience, which correspond with these three kinds of authority. To help us better understand the various kinds or applications of authority, we want to look at the words for obedience in the New Testament and from them determine the nature of the authority necessary to produce the obedience the word requires. If we understand what kind of authority we need to use in any given situation, and what kind of obedience can be expected, we will eliminate most of the problems experienced in exercising authority. And the people under our authority will be spared a lot of unnecessary pain.

TASK AUTHORITY

The purpose of task authority is to accomplish a specific job under a designated leader. The obedience necessary here is the responsibility to follow. This kind of authority quickly molds a group into a single unit - the best authority for emergencies. One of the jobs I did in college was to drive an ambulance. When I started out I was shocked to find out that the driver of the ambulance was in charge of the scene until all the victims are removed from the vehicles involved. At that point it reverts to the police, sheriff or highway patrol, depending on jurisdiction. As a 20-year-old driver on his first response to a serious accident, I found myself out of my depth in being asked to give directions to very experienced firemen and highway patrol officers. It did get easier with time.

The Greek word for this kind of obedience is *peitharcheo*, which means "to obey one in authority." Paul used this word to instruct Titus to obey magistrates

(Titus 3:1). This represents the positional authority a policeman carries when he pulls a car over and gives the driver a ticket for speeding. It is a positional authority, an authority without relationship. Since this kind of authority is not concerned with the relationships, it has limited use in the church.

Authority of this kind comes with a "get it done" mentality. When we renovated our church facility, we did it all with volunteers. Dan, one of our leaders, had a job that allowed him to give a substantial part of his time to getting us ready for each workday. He purchased materials, found the tools needed and planned the jobs to be done. We gave him the authority to get it done. Whenever volunteers would show up, Dan would assign the task and give them everything they would need to finish the job. He was the boss, and he did it well.

Early on in the project he began to wear a Pink Panther baseball cap around the job site. It became a great joke, but it also became a symbol of a particular kind of authority. Any time the pink hat approached, everyone got busy. Not long after the project finished we asked Dan to step into eldership. One day as a part of the process of his development into this new role, he came to me and said he felt he needed to burn the pink hat. He realized that as he stepped into a different sphere, it would require a different kind of authority. The directive, abrupt style that worked well to bring volunteers together would now be replaced with an authority built on relationship and trust that would win the hearts of those he led.

In spiritual terms, *peitharcheo* recognizes the Lordship of Christ and His right to direct us without explanation. Luke used this word in Acts when the high priest told the apostles that they could no longer preach in the name of Jesus. Peter's answer was *we must obey God rather than men* (Acts 5:29). God's authority is the only real absolute spiritual authority. What He says we must do and He is not required to give any explanation. I suspect that this was the kind of authority that Mary used at the wedding feast when she said to the servants, *Whatever He says to you, do it* (John 2:5).

TEACHING AUTHORITY

The second kind of authority occurs much more frequently in the church context. The purpose of this delegated authority is for a person to learn how to do something with the responsibility of asking questions in order to learn. The New Testament word for this kind of obedience is *peitho,* which means "to be persuaded by or to win over." Obedience to this authority comes from understanding the reason and purpose behind instructions. To exercise authority of this kind, the leader must be willing to earn the respect and trust of those they lead. Authority in the church comes from Jesus, but the leader must do more than just present truth. They must also be open to discussion, answer questions and establish a relationship that in the end validates their authority.

The writer of Hebrews used this word when he wrote, "obey your leaders." Authority in the church is much more often a teaching authority than a task authority. In fact applying task authority to teaching situations rarely produces good fruit; rather, it results in someone repeating 'parrot-fashion' the things they have been told, with no life in it. This does not mean that we should never obey until we understand everything. But as we begin to obey and have questions, we know there is opportunity for discussion and greater understanding.

Most of the authority in the church fits into this category. When we give someone a job, we have delegated to him or her a measure of positional authority. But over time if they do not earn the trust or respect of the people, the people will vote with their feet and soon the leader has no one to lead. This idea of earning trust is in keeping with the word we are dealing with. *Peitho* is related to *pisteuo* (trust). The former implies an obedience that is produced by the latter; so, obedience is born out of a trust placed in those who lead. Therefore, whether you teach, administer, or lead a small group, the best way you can exercise authority is to earn the trust of the people you lead.

Often we have people come to us and want a title or position in the hopes that in having a title people will follow them. The problem with this mindset is that it undermines the principle of earning trust and respect. Any delegated authority is dependent on the transition being made from positional authority (given at the time of delegation) to earned respect, which comes as the relationship grows. Leadership authority in the body functions without title. Why? Because people are drawn to the anointing, and they begin to trust and respect the authority in the individual long before that person is put in a position of responsibility.

TRANSFORMATIVE AUTHORITY

The purpose of the third category of authority is not what a person learns to do but what a person learns to be. This kind of authority is concerned with character change and motivation, particularly when a spiritual or ethical law is at issue. The essence of moral behavior can be described as the free response of the will to truth that has registered on the conscience. Only when we respond to the demands made by our conscience, are we engaged in moral behavior. If we alter our actions or attitudes for any other reason (be it prudent or socially demanding), *it is conformity rather than moral response and is ultimately only a reaction to external pressure.*

To understand the principle here, ask a simple question: "Do I drive at the speed limit?" If the answer is yes, then you are engaging in moral behavior because you believe that the speed limit is the law and that it should be obeyed. If, however, your normal driving speed is five or ten miles an hour over the limit, what happens when you see a patrol car? The instinctive reaction is to slow down. Why? So you will not get a ticket. This kind of response to authority is mere conformity to external pressure and has no impact on the long-term behavior. This is what happens when task authority is used in a spiritual situation; it will produce **legalism**. It will create either conformity or rebellion, but not life. The law alone is powerless to truly change us because, *the letter kills, but the Spirit gives life* (2 Cor. 3:6).

The Greek word for obedience to transformative authority is *hupakouo*, which means "to listen under, to attend, or to submit." Notice first, that the obedience is initiated by the person seeking to follow and not by the leader. If we want to change behavior, we must position ourselves in a place of submission to someone who can help us, so that the behavior we want to address will be impacted. Paul uses this word when he tells the Roman church that the goal of his apostleship was to bring about an *obedience of faith* (Rom. 1:5). Placing ourselves in position to receive from another requires an exercise in faith. This is where spiritual fathers and mothers in the faith are so needed.

The exercise of transformative authority is based on the leader's character and experience. These traits give the leader the ability to influence and mentor others because proven character builds trust. To exercise this kind of spiritual authority, the leader must walk in integrity and openness with the people he or she serves. The willingness to be vulnerable and honest about both successes and failures creates the environment for real transformation to take place. Transformative authority is not dependent on position or title because it is relational, based on true acceptance of one another.

Another important element is that change does not happen from the outside in but from the inside out. The goal is to train people to become *obedient from the heart* (Rom. 6:17). The word obedient here is our word hupakouo. Real change comes when we willingly place ourselves in a position which makes us accountable, giving someone the right to exercise his or her authority and help us learn how to begin *doing the will of God from the heart* (Eph. 6:6).

Paul uses this word for obedience when he tells the Philippians that he is pleased that they have, *obeyed, not as in my presence only, but now much more in my absence...* (Phil. 2:12). Spiritual authority has as its goal that each member of the body is brought to maturity so that he or she does what is right whether they are being watched or not.

The weight of transformative authority is truth in practice. The truth we live out defines the transformative authority that we carry. Our life then becomes the validation of the truth. This allows the leader to teach people to "hear the truth" and faithfully obey its demands on their conscience. Hearing with our conscience produces real change, a change that comes from our hearts.

TEAM LEADERSHIP

Understanding the three kinds of authority is critical in a leadership team. Operating effectively in a team setting requires a special kind of leader. Strong authoritarian leadership may produce followers but not a team. The authority needed to build a team must create a safe atmosphere in which real openness and honesty are encouraged. For this reason task authority has limited application. There are a few kinds of teams involved in emergency or military activity where task authority would be appropriate. The transformative authority we just discussed, although crucial to the development of individuals, does not necessarily fit the need of team leadership.

So, the kind of authority best suited for the development of team ministry is authority that earns the respect and loyalty of the other team members. This means that the authority of the leader must be received and recognized by the team for it to be effective. Imposed authority will always cause insecurity in the team members. Leaders will earn the respect of the team by operating with a consultative style that leaves plenty of room for the ideas and creativity of the team to be utilized. Therefore, in the environment of a team the leader must be secure enough to allow the team members to share their hearts freely.

If you haven't read the book *Good to Great,* it is a good read. Collins studied companies that had excelled in the business world and, as a part of the study, he defined a new kind of leadership that made these exceptional organizations work. He called them level 5 leaders and he made several startling observations. In his words these kinds of leaders *"displayed an unusual mix of intense determination and profound humility."*[9] He went on to say he discovered that for these exceptional team leaders their *"personal ego and individual financial gain are not as important as the long-term benefit of the team."*

Jesus modeled this kind of authority. We gladly submit to Him not because He demands it but because He won our trust. As an old hymn says, He who lives to be my King once died to be my Savior.

CHAPTER 13
CONFLICT
OPPORTUNITY FOR GROWTH

Everyone must be quick to hear, slow to speak and slow to anger
JAMES 1:19

Conflict is certainly not one of our favorite words. Most of us do not relish it but, unfortunately, conflict is essential to relationship growth and an intrinsic component of leadership development. We wish it could be avoided for sure! However, if we commit to building team ministry, then conflict will surface as part of the process whether we like it or not. In truth, no relationship of any value has ever been built without some measure of conflict emerging in the process. Meaning that if we learn to deal with conflict constructively, it will deepen and strengthen the relationships in a leadership team.

Jesus sometimes provoked conflict with the religious leaders to get them to think beyond the limitations of their expectations. In doing so, Jesus sanctioned conflict for the purpose of exposing areas of blindness. From His encounter with Nicodemus we can see that His goal was not conflict, but the revelation and freedom that follows.

The truth is that without conflict we will not grow. But how we deal with the contention will determine both the quality and depth of relationships within the team. Teams that have worked through the process of resolving internal conflict are always healthier, stronger and more effective than teams who live with unresolved issues. The good news is that by resolving conflict successfully, we can solve many of the underlying problems that provoked the disagreement in the first place. If we are unable to resolve the issues, we end up avoiding the struggle and limiting our growth.

This does not make avoiding conflict necessarily wrong; there are legitimate reasons to leave things alone. But do not leave things unresolved too long or the issues will begin to multiply. In the development of a leadership team, if we consistently avoid conflict, we bypass essential stages of growth, leaving the team immature. The long-term effect of avoiding relationship issues within the team stunts the growth of the ministry.

Relationships in the team are adversely affected by avoiding conflict because deception and pretense have been introduced. We still feel like we are going in the same direction, but not really together. The team will not achieve their goals until we step back and deal with the real issues. When we consistently fail to resolve conflict, we communicate that we do not care enough to deal with the issues. This devaluing of the others in the team has serious impact on the effectiveness of the team and, although it may appear to work in the short term, it will eventually trip us up.

Sally and I once planted a church in an unfamiliar city with a couple we did not know well. It was a challenging situation made worse because of the deep insecurity in their lives. In the process of getting to know them, all had seemed to go well. But as soon as the demands of leading a diverse group of individuals began to settle on our friends, insecurities began to surface. The loving, supportive demeanor that had characterized the early stages of building our relationship vanished as Hyde replaced Jekyll. We should have seen the warning signs, but we did not recognize it until it was too late.

I first noticed that the husband just could not listen; as long as he was talking, everything would be fine. But if I had counsel to bring him, he would use doubt or criticism to deflect the conversation away from himself. He lived in a world where, if anyone else succeeded, he seemed to feel that he lost, making it impossible for him to compliment or celebrate another leader. My friend simply had to maintain control, meaning that he micromanaged everything under his care. The frustration this created in the rest of the team was not pretty.

DEALING WITH INSECURITY

Insecurity is a significant roadblock to developing relationships in leadership. We all have encountered it, but sometimes find it a little difficult to quantify. On some level we all have insecurities but, after many years in ministry and countless meetings with church leaders, I can say with confidence that dealing with insecure leadership has proved one of the greatest challenges we have faced. Insecurity operates like an insidious cancer that eats away at a leader's confidence and produces an array of issues that, if left unchecked, will divide and destroy a leadership team.

Some form of insecurity lies at the root of almost every leadership conflict we have ever been involved in. Tragically, what makes this even more devastating is that insecure people find it very difficult to receive counsel or correction; this makes it nearly impossible to resolve the underlying issues. Without recognition of the damage their insecurity is causing and without true repentance from the self-focus, the conflict is unlikely to get resolved. We just learn to live with it, while recognizing that it has put severe limitations on the effectiveness of the leadership team.

Insecurity can be defined as uncertainty or anxiety about oneself, a lack of confidence. Alternately, it is the state of feeling open to danger or threat - lack of protection. This second meaning aligns with the original Latin meaning of "unsafe." When we feel insecure we feel unsafe at some level. Everything we do becomes centered on finding and maintaining a safe environment for ourselves.

This means that insecure leaders always focus on themselves and the safety of their position, their ideas, their pulpit, etc.

Solomon wrote that, *the name of the Lord is a strong tower; the righteous runs into it and is safe* (Prov. 18:10). David felt something similar when he wrote, *Uphold me that I may be safe, that I may have regard for Your statutes continually* (Ps. 119:117). These two leaders recognized the need to feel safe, but they drew their safety from the right source. If we try to draw our safety or security from the responses of people around us, we will never feel secure. If we go to the Source, we will always be safe.

The Hebrew word *safe* means, "to be high" and frequently has the connotation of security.[10] The idea is that of being too high for capture or to be set securely on high. It also has the meaning that safety comes as a result of being exalted or placed in a position of honor **by God**. When our identity comes from God and not from what people say or think, we find ourselves safe and confident. If our security is in any way associated with how others view us, then we have stepped into a snare called the fear of man. Solomon described this - and its remedy - when he wrote, *the fear of man brings a snare, but he who trusts in the Lord will be exalted* (Prov. 29:25).

In a leadership team, our deep need to be liked, to be affirmed and to be respected as a leader will always war against the need to go deep and be vulnerable in relationships. If we are not careful, the focus of the team will have more to do with how we feel than it does with achieving the goals of the team. **The basic problem with insecurity is that it always exalts self.** When we feel insecure, our self-image is threatened and we set about to protect ourselves from the perceived threat. This makes us almost continually self-focused.

We can see this principle clearly in Matthew chapter 6. Jesus is teaching about where our confidence should focus. He makes the statement that *no man can serve two masters* (Matt. 6:24 KJV). He is speaking of divided loyalty and goes on to say that you *cannot serve God and mammon*. The word *mammon* is Aramaic, meaning "the treasure a person trusts in." It comes from a root meaning "confidence." This gives a twist to the meaning, with the idea of "that which can be trusted" or *"that which brings safety."[11]* The idea is that the accumulation of possessions gives us our self-security. Mammon then is materialism with a purpose of providing security. **We either trust God or that which gives security to self.**

We cannot have it both ways; we cannot serve God and our need for security at the same time. We will either find our security in the broken system of self-protection or we will trust God with our life and find our security and safety in Him. Building our security separate from our identity in Him always has us focused on ourselves and self-focus will never give us security.

It has been shown in sports that if a person concentrates too much on their performance, it actually deteriorates. We are not designed to be self-focused; we were created to love and support one another. The ability to do this comes when we discover the security available to us as we press into the promises of God who causes - *all things to work together for good...* (Rom. 8:28). And then a few verses later He promises to give us everything else that we need and that includes assurance of safety (Rom. 8:32). When we walk in our calling and remain secure in our identity, we have confidence that He provides the safety.

DEALING WITH CONFLICT

Resolution should be the goal in any conflict situation. We have already mentioned the danger of avoiding conflict, but there are other ways that we can react. One of the more subtle consequences of not dealing with conflict correctly is to allow ourselves to be deflected by it. At times we do not even realize it has happened until we look back and see that we have been diverted from our mission and are no longer on course. Other times we retreat from conflict as a reaction to bullying, anger or aggression on the part of one or more people involved. Other times it just takes too much energy, so we withdraw rather than face issues. The most damaging pattern is when we react to conflict by outbursts of anger or frustration, which damage relationships, making it harder to resolve the issues. If not quickly dealt with, leaders tend to draw battle lines and the whole atmosphere of the church suffers.

KEYS TO SUCCESSFUL RESOLUTION

The heart of successfully resolving a conflict is simply learning to work together. We learn to work together by dealing with real issues in a manner that builds our confidence in each other's value. The goal is to learn to resolve conflict in such a way that both parties feel validated. When we do this successfully, we make progress together and the relationship goes deeper. Resolution is the only way of dealing with conflict that produces lasting fruit and releases us fully into our destiny. There are also several other benefits to the process.

An obvious plus is increased understanding. The discussion needed in order to resolve conflict increases our awareness of each other's needs and gives insight into how we can get our needs met without undermining those of the other person. We also get to know ourselves better by coming to terms with our own strengths and weaknesses. Conflict pushes us to know and understand our priorities, and it increases our ability to communicate effectively with others. Finally, when conflict is resolved effectively, people develop stronger mutual respect and a renewed faith in their ability to work together. This is an essential key to going deeper and developing intimacy in our relationships.

LEARN TO INITIATE

Whether the contention comes from offense or just a simple misunderstanding, whose responsibility is it to make the first move toward reconciliation: the offender or the offended? Jesus answers this in Matthew. *Therefore you are presenting your offering at the altar, and there remember that your brother has something against you, leave your offering there before the altar and go; first be reconciled to your brother, and then come and present your offering* (Matt. 5:23, 24). And then again He says that, *If your brother sins against you, go and show him his fault, just between the two of you. If he listens to you, you have won your brother over* (Matt. 18:15 NIV).

CONFLICT OPPORTUNITY FOR GROWTH

In the first verse, Jesus instructs the offender to go and make it right and in the second passage He tells the offended to make it right. So the answer is **both**! Both parties to a conflict have the responsibility to take the initiative and go to the other person in an effort to make things right. Too many times we have watched leaders waiting for someone else to make the first move, when in fact it was their responsibility to take the initiative and bring resolution. Having established the principle of initiating resolution, let's look at some principles that govern the process.

LEARN TO VALUE RELATIONSHIPS

In the U.S. individualism and self-reliance are core values that come from our naturalistic and humanistic worldview. The resulting focus on personal development and satisfaction at the expense of corporate unity makes it difficult to build and sustain deep friendships. This weakness in our culture means that we need to **learn** to value relationships. *Above all, keep fervent in your love for one another, because love covers a multitude of sins* (1 Pet. 4:8).

God is relational! He created us to have relationship with Him and the whole plan of salvation restores the relationship that had been lost in the fall. This restoration has both a vertical and horizontal component. Not only is our vertical relationship with God restored, the cross also released reconciliation in our earthly relationships.

God puts high valve on individuals; therefore we must treat people with great value. The value of that person is the value of Jesus' blood, which makes them priceless and determines the way that we should relate and interact. Scripture makes this clear when it says, *If someone says, 'I love God,' and hates his brother, he is a liar; for the one who does not love his brother whom he has seen, cannot love God whom he has not seen* (1 John 4:20).

The value we place on the relationship determines how hard we work at resolving issues. Quite literally, we will seek to resolve a conflict with someone in direct proportion to the value we place on the relationship we have with them.

Maturity requires placing a high priority on maintaining good relationships and being diligent to keep them healthy. This means that we are to treat people in a way that shows and builds respect by consistently responding in a constructive manner even under pressure. There are three principles that keep us honest in this.

To begin with, we must put the relationship first. People are not disposable; this means we must never try to correct people beyond the level of the relationship. The relationship must become more important to us than our need to be right. Our spiritual dad would often say, "You cannot drive a tank over a plywood bridge." If you did, the bridge would collapse and the relationship would be lost. We at times try to bring truth to people without having sufficient depth of relationship to sustain our fellowship.

Second, we must keep people and problems separate. Recognize that in many cases the other person is not just "being difficult." Many times real and valid differences lie behind conflict, differences that need to be addressed and resolved. By separating the problem from the person, real issues can be discussed without damaging the relationship. Nelson Mandela, one of my heroes once said, *"I defeated my opponents without dishonoring them."*[12] Even though he deeply disagreed with the positions of apartheid, he was able to challenge the system and yet treat the people involved with honor.

Finally, be willing to seriously consider their point of view. Sometimes all people want *is to be heard, to feel their viewpoint is important*. That means we never start by saying "you're wrong." Rather, we try to imagine ourself in their shoes and look for areas of agreement. Ask the Holy Spirit to help us see what they see; there's power in the words, "Yes, I see what you're saying." By agreeing, we gradually break down the anger barrier.

LEARN TO LISTEN

Sometimes one of the hardest things for us to do is to listen but, if we want to learn to resolve conflict, it is one of the most important skills we must master.

After his meeting with Jesus, Nicodemus reminded the Pharisees of the need to listen before making a judgment. *Our Law does not judge a man unless it first hears from him and knows what he is doing, does it?* (John 7:51). So, if we find ourselves in a situation of conflict, we must discipline ourselves to listen first; talk second. Get in the right frame of mind; determine in advance that we are going to give them our full attention. When we listen to them first, we communicate value and build a bridge for reconciliation.

To solve a problem effectively we have to understand where the other person is coming from before defending our own position. Listen for ways to validate them, not just for what is wrong. Everyone has something valuable to say. So listen with respect; concentrate, focus on understanding what is being said. Do not plan the answer while we are listening, if we do, we are not really giving them our full attention.

BE AN ACTIVE LISTENER

Listening requires involvement, not "stony silence." If we want people to feel heard, use 'encouragers' in the conversation -"I hear you" "uh huh" "yes." It lets the person know we have engaged with them. Body language while listening is also important. Keep our eyes on the person rather than looking around the room. When the person is speaking, lean towards them, keep arms and hands open and relaxed. The goal is to make them feel heard and that we respect their point of view.

Active listening involves engaging with the other person, but do not interrupt; it is so easy to do. If we want to see the situation resolved, we must let them finish before we speak. When we interrupt, it makes people feel we are not listening and that we do not value them. Practice patience; give them our full attention. Remember, it takes some people a long time to say what they need to say.

THERE IS MORE THAN ONE TRUTH!

Another key to listening comes with accepting that there is more than one truth. Many elements affect the understanding of what is true concerning a situation. To start with, there is what we said versus *what we think we said*. Then, there is *what they heard* complicated with issues like missing or different information and their perception of circumstances. Add to that, assumptions made about the situation which are then filtered through past experience. To the best of our ability what we believe is the truth. But often it is only partial because lack of (or improper) information has distorted our understanding. The result is often a communication breakdown. Remember, our failure to give others information does not make them wrong. Unfortunately, when we do this, we end up judging each other for not having all the facts.

So when listening, we need to strive to see the other side by putting ourselves deliberately in their shoes. Pay particular attention to their concerns; by listening carefully you'll hear and understand why the person is adopting his or her position. To do this we must deal with our pride, perceptions and assumptions. We must set aside our own insecurities, because our own self-protection always impedes progress.

Remember that on the way to Lazarus's resurrection Jesus stopped and *"troubled Himself"* to weep with Mary (John 11:33). No doubt He knew there would be a resurrection, but He stopped and related to the emotion of Mary's pain. So as you listen, trouble yourself. Ask internal questions to help yourself focus: "What do they know that I do not? What are they not saying? What are they reluctant to say?" Always remember that those involved will by nature only see their side, so make sure you hear them before you try to answer. Remember, *He who gives an answer before he hears, it is folly and shame to him* (Prov. 18:13).

GUARD EMOTIONAL RESPONSES.

Conflict creates emotions and feelings that can form barriers to communication. Get to know the words that trigger emotional responses in us and do not get distracted by them. We will not be listening if we are upset or agitated. Pay particular attention when the other person says something we do not agree with – this is when we are most vulnerable. Guarding emotions in this way does not mean dismissing them. We must acknowledge emotions, because facts alone - however rational - cannot fully resolve conflict. The way people perceive the facts of a situation is colored by their emotions. It's no good denying emotions; so, make an effort to see the situation the way the other person does and acknowledge their emotions before endeavoring to move beyond them.

LEARN TO RESPOND

Having listened to the other person and heard their heart, it is time to respond. The way we do this will either pour healing balm on the wound or gas on the fire. *A gentle answer turns away wrath, but a harsh word stirs up anger* (Prov. 15:1 NIV). So, do not become defensive or justify your position, and do not play the blame game. Rather, look for what is true even in their criticism. Treat the other person as having great value; in this way we create an environment that establishes good will before discussing issues. One of the best ways to do this is to start by taking responsibility for the relational breakdown.

BE WILLING TO ADMIT YOU ARE WRONG

Taking personal responsibility is strength; so as you listen, deliberately look for the areas where you failed, then be quick to apologize. This sets the example and shows maturity. It also inspires the other person to respond, though watch your motive; apology must be genuine.

Whatever you do, do not raise the stakes. There is a moment when a conflict is either escalated or defused. Watch the words and emotive statements. Rather than saying "You are lying," say, "I did not see it that way." Rather than saying, "You said," say "I thought I heard." One statement attributes motive to the person, while the other opens the door for discussion. We add nothing by attacking the motives of the other person. Let us surround our response with grace and not law. Rather than defending ourselves, yield our rights to God. Walk in forgiveness and never hold a grudge. The greater goal is to understand their position, not convince them of ours.

Part of the process is to give feedback. This may involve repeating in our words what we heard them say, "So what you are saying is…" "I just want to be sure I have understood." Ask questions to clarify, "I would like to understand better how you see this situation." "Please explain to me why this is important to you." Then reverse it. "Let me try to explain how I see things." "Please allow me to explain why this is so important to me."

As we speak to the issue, break the conflict into segments, so that we deal with one issue at a time. If possible, start with areas of agreement. Someone once said that, *"Underneath incompatible positions lay compatible interests."* We believe this provides a primary key for finding resolution. Together we dig for and reach the compatible interests so we can rediscover common ground. To do this we need the Holy Spirit to help us identify and understand how to get there.

CHAPTER 14
TOGETHER
BUILDING TEAMWORK

So that he who sows and he who reaps may rejoice together
JOHN 4:36

Teamwork is God's design to keep leaders from operating in isolation. As we look around the nations, we recognize that the churches that have begun to sustain a revival presence all operate with some form of team leadership. We believe that team is the leadership model necessary to bring in the harvest. For this reason we challenge every church to begin to think team as they examine their leadership. We also challenge every leadership to give themselves to building and maintaining lasting relationships in order to facilitate teamwork.

One only needs to look at Billy Graham and his team to see that this is possible. Many of the key players in the association have been together for years. They have walked together, wept together and rejoiced together. At the same time the accountability they have in place has helped them avoid the kinds of scandal that have disabled other ministries. Cliff Barrows at the 60th anniversary celebration stated that:

It's a marvelous thing to be knit together in heart. I've been with Bill 65 years and we've never had one word of disagreement or one argument.

Now that's an amazing thing. That's his grace and God's goodness and I praise Him for it. To have the fellowship of the team means everything, because we encourage one another. We are so privileged to be co-laborers together with Christ. Bill has a great heart for team ministry and BGEA is a ministry built on a team relationship.[13]

These kinds of sustained relationships require a revelation that we belong together. Belonging is what brings us together. On the day of Pentecost we are told that, *they were all together in one place* (Acts 2:1). Belonging got them to the upper room but **together** created the atmosphere for the Holy Spirit to fall. For team leadership to function we need both a sense of belonging and a feeling of togetherness.

We are placed together to be a team. Together describes how we live our lives with one another. The phrase "*one another*" occurs 106 times in the New Testament and covers almost every area of life and relationship. Reading the context of the *one anothers* in scripture gives us a glimpse into the breadth of God's design and intention for our relationships. The idea of being together requires that we must first be <u>with</u> one another; this gives us our fellowship. We are also to move <u>toward</u> one another, which means that our heart response is inclined to go deeper in relationships, rather than to pull back. Finally, to be together we must give ourselves for one another so that our actions become consistently unselfish.

God places us together with one another in teams for sharing life. We read of the early church that, *all those who had believed were together and had all things in common* (Acts 2:44). We all know that it is possible to be in the same room with other people and not really be together. If we are among people, yet thinking about ourselves, we are not really together. Self focus wars against togetherness, because our life together requires a focus on others. If we are truly together, all our needs will be met, but only when our focus is on one another.

A couple of verses later we get a glimpse into the quality of fellowship they enjoyed. *Day by day continuing with one mind in the temple, and breaking bread from house to house, they were taking their meals together with gladness and sincerity of heart...* (Acts 2:46). Someone once said, "Friendship isn't about who you've known the longest. It's about who walked into your life, said 'I'm here for you' and proved it."

God places us together in teams for a purpose. When people with common purpose come together in a team they will find unity. When the pressure begins to come on the disciples, we read that *when they had prayed, the place where they had gathered together was shaken, and they were all filled with the Holy Spirit and began to speak the word of God with boldness* (Acts 4:31). Mission always precedes true unity. We are together not just to meet needs but so that the world will know our hope... that there is a people who will live unselfishly. When the world sees a people united by God's unconditional love working together to make Jesus King, they will respond.

We are placed together in a team to compliment one another. Jesus said, *already he who reaps is receiving wages and is gathering fruit for life eternal; so that he who sows and he who reaps may rejoice together* (John 4:36). We have different functions but the same joy. When I am concerned about my gift, I am not together. When I want to be recognized, I am not together. The revelation of the diversity necessary to bring in the harvest will give us a desperate need to find each other and work together in complementary relationship.

We are placed together in team to encourage one another. At the resurrection we read that *The two were running together; and the other disciple ran ahead faster than Peter and came to the tomb first* (John 20:4). When we belong, we act together toward a common goal. This common focus as we act together creates a synergy that causes us to become even more productive. Imagine Peter and John provoking each other as they try to get to the tomb first. That's the healthy competition that encourages us to go further.

FINAL THOUGHTS

For those who have begun to implement team ministry in the local church, we offer four suggestions. In examining the most effective leadership teams we have encountered, we have identified four traits that set them apart. First, they exhibit a fivefold understanding; second, they focus on body ministry; third, they seek to be multicultural and finally, they are deliberately multigenerational. Let's examine why each of these is important to teamwork.

MAKE THE TEAM FIVEFOLD

Churches learning to sustain the awakening all evidence some measure of team ministry that represents more than one ministry gift. Specifically, they have an understanding of five-fold ministry and its application to team ministry. When we operate with only one of the ministry gifts touching the church, it is like trying to play a guitar with only one string. No matter how well tuned the string is, it's isolation sets limits on how much music can be played. And with only one string, harmony is out of reach. The more strings we add to the instrument the more effective it becomes at fulfilling its purpose.

Danny Silk who works with Bill Johnson at Bethel asserts that "the fivefold design for leadership is obviously a team design; so the one-man show version of church leadership is clearly not an expression of it, and neither is the bureaucratic, homogeneous, 'everyone can do the job' style of leadership."[14] The goal for the church in this hour is to walk the balance between a hierarchical, authoritarian leadership structure and egalitarian impasse. Awakened churches exercise great spiritual authority but walk in grace and humility which allows other voices to be heard and the gifts and callings in the body to thrive.

MAKE THE TEAM BODY MINISTRY FOCUSED

Effective leadership teams in this season of awakening focus on releasing the body to do the work of the ministry. Paul tells the Ephesians that the ministry gifts were given for the maturing of the body to do the work of ministry. Gone is the time when we all focused on our own gift or ministry. This season of harvest means that the whole body must be equipped and released to do the work.

A body focus proves necessary for the cohesive operation of a team. If the team members embrace this, there is no thought as to whose turn it is; rather, the focus is on raising up and releasing as many people as possible into ministry. If we were asked to give a distinguishing mark of a man or woman called to five-fold ministry, we would say that it is the joy they feel when someone else succeeds. If we cannot find satisfaction in the release of others, there is an insecurity in us that needs to go to the cross.

MAKE THE TEAM INTENTIONALLY DIVERSE

The Church exists for mission - a mission that transcends every cultural, gender, and socioeconomic barrier and shapes the activities of the Church. As we build relational unity focused on mission, authentic diverse community will emerge. This diversity displays to the world the multifaceted glory of God.

The triumph of the Jerusalem council came with a decision that "different" was not wrong (Acts 15). The apostles and elders led by the Spirit acknowledged unity in diversity, recognizing that the key issue centered on the mission and not the traditions. The Church today finds it easy to believe that the form and not mission has eternal significance. Only when we embrace the mission of seeing the world transformed will our vision be broad enough to sustain real diversity.

Remember the body metaphor from chapter 4 which highlighted our uniqueness and unity. Each member of the body has unique roles and functions, meaning that the whole cannot operate without their interdependent supply. While all the parts may not be equal in gift, they are all essential; even *those parts of the body that seem to be weaker are indispensable* (1 Cor. 12:22 NIV). When we apply this to cultural diversity, the body image highlights the interaction and interdependence of different cultures for the common good of the whole. The purpose of this diversity in terms of mission is for the world to see the church bridging the deep divisions in society with the power of love.

MAKE THE TEAM MULTIGENERATIONAL

Effective team ministry in this season of harvest must include a move toward multigenerational leadership. The transition from Elijah to Elisha demonstrates that a father's blessing is available for those who pursue correctly. In the natural, things tend to deteriorate and while this may prove true of institutions, it does not follow for the people of God. Anyone who pursues God wholeheartedly has the opportunity for increase. Elijah served as a bold prophet with a rough disposition and great anointing. In the end, however, his life was remembered for his investment in the next generation. The prophet Malachi looked back to this relationship as the defining bridge between generations, which would be restored at the end of the age (Mal. 4:6). In a time when things are out of order, divided, and broken almost beyond repair, the spirit of Elijah would be poured out. Elijah invested himself into Elisha, and treated him as a son. Elisha in return was moved to give his heart to his father.

Elisha followed him, learning servanthood, persistence and patience. When the transition time came, it was not enough for Elisha to simply pick up the mantle of Elijah; he wanted the double portion blessing reserved for the oldest son (2 Kings 2:13).[15] The prerequisite to this transition, however, is that the two generations must align themselves correctly. Elijah's response to Elisha that he had asked a hard thing (1 Kings 2:10) does not refer only to receiving the anointing but to the difficulty of staying in correct alignment with the older generation. The next generation will find the father's blessing out of reach without developing a relational loyalty to the older generation. In fact there was another servant who did not go the distance (1 Kings 19:3). He looked at the trip through the desert to Sinai and let Elijah talk him out of going. When faced with the same decision, Elisha chose to go the distance and received the blessing.

The Spirit of Elijah is being released. Through faithfulness, obedience and loyalty, a new generation of sons and daughters are emerging. They look for spiritual mothers and fathers ready to join hearts in the task of reaching the nations. As we walk together the anointing and spiritual authority they need is being transferred to them and the double-portion anointing will be released. For this generation, settling for simple continuity has proved unsatisfying; they want more. If they will learn to pursue God and walk in correct relational alignment with others, God will not disappoint.

INCOMPLETE BY DESIGN

ENDNOTES

1. Kevin J. Connors, *The Church in the New Testament,* Bible Temple Publishing Portland Oregon, 1989, P 92.

2. Novatian, *A Treatise of Novatian Concerning the Trinity*, Post-Nicene Library 10 vols. Grand Rapids: Wm. B. Eerdmans Publishing Co., 1987. Chapter XXIX, section 251.

3. Sam Matthews, *Apostolic Teams: Penetrating the Nations: A Strategic 5-fold Ministry Model for the 21st Centur,* Shawnee: Matthews Publishing, 2001, 77.

4. Philip Mohabir, *Hands of Jesus: Reaching Out to the Nations, Bringing the Church to Maturity, Equipping the Saints for Ministry, Growing the Body to be a corporate Entity,* Denmark: Powerhouse Publishing, 2003, 318.

5. Encyclopedia Britannica, http://www.britannica.com/EBchecked/topic/177746/Ecclesia

6. H. Vinson Synan, *The Holiness Pentecostal Tradition,*www.charismanews.com/opinion/42478-3-keys-to-sustaining-revival-20-years-after-the-toronto-blessing

7. Jon Ronson, *Catch Me if You Can: Getting Religious with Nicky Gumbel*, Article on the Alpha Course, The Guardian, Oct 20, 2000.

8. Lindley Lodge was a training facility in Masham, North Yorkshire. A special thanks to Phil and the other trainers who were part of Ripon Christian Fellowship, I am forever grateful for the part you played in helping me become a better leader.

9. Jim Collins, *Good to Great: Why some Companies Make the Leap… and Others Don't*, New York, Harper Collins 2001, Chapter 2.

10. Brown Driver Briggs Hebrew Lexicon.

11. James Hastings, ed.; Encyclopedia of Religion and Ethics, New York, Scribners, 1908–1921 Volume 8:374.

12. Nelson Mandela, *Long Walk To Freedom: The Autobiography of Nelson Mandela*, Boston, New York, London, Back, Bay Books, Little Brown and Company, 1995, 142.

13. Janet Chismar, Billy Graham Glorifies God for 60 Years of Ministry, Billy Graham Evangelistic Assoc. Nov 17 2010 http://billygraham.org/story/billy-graham-glorifies-god-for-60-years-of-ministry/

14. Danny Silk, *Culture of Honor: Sustaining a Supernatural Environment* (Shippensburg, PA: Destiny Image, 2009), 75.

15. Kiel and Delitzsch, *Commentary on the Old Testament, Volume 2, The Second Book of Kings*, 293. The authors view this request for the double portion as a reference to Deut. 21:17, the double portion blessing reserved for the firstborn son. Elisha therefore makes his request as a son and asks for the double portion inheritance reserved for the eldest son from his spiritual father Elijah.

KEEP THE FIRE BURNING

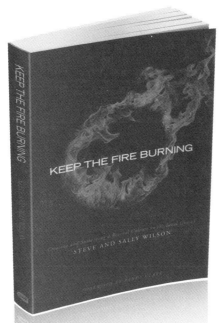

WHO SAYS REVIVAL HAS TO STOP

Keep the Fire Burning: *Creating and Sustaining a Revival Culture in the Local Church,* is one of the most thorough books on revival in print today, a blueprint for birthing and sustaining revival. Steve and Sally Wilson bring a wisdom and clarity to the subject of revival that is not just from theory but from their experience of living in a revival culture. They have cultivated a personal revival culture over a lifetime and successfully empowered others to live a revival lifestyle as well. Steve and Sally begin by establishing that it is possible to create a revival culture anywhere and that it can be sustained. It is not a seasonal event. They help us see that the reason revivals are seasonal is due to earthly causes and not because God stopped them. They explore what needs to be valued to sustain revival beyond the usual three to four years of past American revivals. As you read Keep the Fire Burning, let the Wilson's experiences and impartation propel you and your church into your supernatural destiny as a world changer.

INCOMPLETE
BY DESIGN